Now Here's a Funny Thing

By the same author

Let's Go Somewhere
Armchair Cricket
Stumped for a Tale
The Wit of Cricket
All About Cricket
It's Been a Lot of Fun
It's a Funny Game . . .
Rain Stops Play
Chatterboxes

BRIAN JOHNSTON

NOW HERE'S A FUNNY THING

Methuen

First published in 1984
by Methuen London Ltd
11 New Fetter Lane, London EC4P 4EE
Copyright © 1984 Brian Johnston
Printed in Great Britain
Richard Clay (The Chaucer Press) Ltd.
Bungay, Suffolk

ISBN 0 413 56340 5

Acknowledgements

I would like to acknowledge my gratitude to the
following: all the music-hall artists who have
unwittingly supplied so much material for this
book; the many friends and acquaintances who
know that I always like to hear the latest story, and
usually tell it to me; and Joe Fagg for allowing me
to use some of the very funny material which he
sends out regularly to the customers of Fagg's Fleet
in Ashford. Finally, I would like to thank
Christopher Falkus, not only for his
encouragement and friendly advice in helping me
to write the book, but also for his appreciative
laughter at the results, which has given me
confidence that the stories and jokes *are* as funny as
I thought they were.

CONTENTS

PREFACE

I have always enjoyed laughter. Either laughing at other people's jokes or stories, or trying to make them laugh at mine. In fact I started trying to be funny early on at school. Our history master said: 'I will now tell you something about Henry's wife – Henrietta.'

'Did he really?' I piped up from the back of the class. A dreadful joke but it was quick and spontaneous and got a belly laugh at the time. It's a marvellously rewarding sound, only equalled by the groan which greets a good pun.

All my life I have never been able to resist the chance of making a joke or a pun. Like a batsman who hits out at every ball, only a few reach the boundary. But at least those few which *do* score a laugh are my own invention. Thousands of other people are doing the same thing, and so jokes are created by people's spontaneous wit or humour. They are then told and retold until a standard joke is born. But who makes up the stories? These are not spontaneous and have to be worked out in detail. Good stories spread like wildfire, but their origins remain a mystery.

There is no copyright on jokes and funny stories. Morecambe and Wise freely admit that they pinched Abbott and Costello's gags when building up their act. We after-dinner speakers know only too well that many of the diners scribble down the best of our material on the back of their menus. In fact Frank Bough told me that he once stopped in the middle of a speech he was giving and asked a scribbling diner: 'Am I going too fast for you?'

When I began to live in London during the early and mid-thirties I used to haunt the music-halls, usually the Palladium, Holborn Empire and Chelsea Palace. I especially enjoyed the stand-up and cross-talk comics and unashamedly noted down the best of their jokes and stories. Then after the war, when I joined the BBC, I had a tremendous bit of luck. The Outside Broadcast Department was

1

responsible for a 'live' broadcast every Tuesday night direct from the stage of one of the many music-halls then still dotted around the country. It was my job to select where we went and what artists we used. And, even more important, I also had to censor some of the broader jokes. In these broadcasts we were using artists as they performed in front of a public audience. There were no special scripts doctored to the BBC's requirements as happened in broadcasts from a studio. This was the raw meat of music-hall and I had a very difficult job trying to please equally the BBC, the theatre audience (who didn't want their comics watered down) and of course the comics themselves. Whenever I asked them to cut out a particularly blue joke for our broadcast, they invariably protested that it was the one which got their biggest laugh. Anyway once again I was involved in the variety world and continued my habit of noting down the best jokes and stories. And I have been doing so ever since.

So this book is a collection of material collected by me over the last fifty years. Old music-hall buffs will recognise the origins of much of it, especially those from my especial favourite, the best timer and stand-up comic ever – Max Miller. But we still don't know where *he* got his stories from. Did he sit down and make them up, or did he pick them up from other people and at chance meetings in pubs, always happy hunting grounds for story swapping?

When deciding on the layout of the book we thought at one time of dividing it up as follows: (1) Stories which you can tell to anyone; (2) Stories which you can tell to *almost* anyone – but not to your maiden aunt!; (3) Stories which should only be told 'when the ladies have left the table'; (4) Stories suitable only for Rugby Club dinners!

I quickly discarded the last option as being too dangerous. Then I came to the conclusion that in this modern, free world it would be best to leave the censorship to the individual reader. So you will find all the jokes and stories under their appropriate subject headings and it will then be up to *you* to choose to whom you tell them.

And the title? Well once again the old music-hall buffs will remember Max Miller – in his white trilby hat, multi-coloured silk plus-fours and jacket, giant-size tie, black and white correspondent's shoes and a wicked twinkle in his eyes. Stepping forward with one foot on the footlights, giving a furtive glance into the wings as if to see whether the manager was listening, beckoning to the audience with his hand and saying: 'Now here's a funny thing....' and off he would go into another outrageous story.

I hope, like *his* audience, you will have lots of belly laughs, and find lots of funny things.

DUMB CHUMS

A buck met an attractive doe in a wood. 'Let's make love', he said. 'It won't take long. Did it?'

Two fleas left a cinema. When they got outside one said to the other: 'Shall we walk or take a dog?'

Two fleas flew out of Robinson Crusoe's hair. 'See you on Friday,' one shouted to the other.

A man sitting in the corner of a railway carriage kept tearing bits out of his newspaper, screwing them into small balls and then throwing them out of the window. The man sitting opposite asked him why he was doing it.

'To keep the elephants away.'

'But there aren't any elephants,' said the other passenger.

'I know. It's very effective, isn't it!'

Five animals were having a drink at a bar, when the barman asked for payment.

The skunk said: 'I've only got one (s)cent.'

The duck added: 'I've only got one bill and I'm not going to break that.'

The deer said: 'I had a buck on me earlier, but it will be some time before I get a little dough.'

The cow mooed: 'Let one of the udders pay.'

The giraffe remarked sadly: 'Well, I guess the high balls are on me.'

'I call my dog Trueman.'
'Why?'
'Because he's got four short legs and his balls swing both ways.'

'I call mine Carpenter.'
'Why?'
'Because he's always doing odd jobs about the house. You should see him make a bolt for the door.'

'Our dog never eats meat.'
'Why not?'
'We never give him any.'

'I've just had to shoot my dog.'
'Was he mad?'
'Well. He wasn't too pleased.'

'My dog's got the coldest nose in London.'
'How do you know that?'
'Whenever he comes into a room all the other dogs sit down.'

'My dog has no nose.'
'How does he smell, then?'
'Terrible.'

'The livery stables have sent me round a horse to ride. It reminds me of Napoleon in exile.'
'How's that?'
'They couldn't have St Helena horse.'

'Do you know why that attractive mare Heartbreak Hill fell at Bechers in last year's Grand National?'
'No. Why did she?'
'She saw Errol Flynn standing the other side of the jump and immediately crossed her legs.'

6

'Has your dog got a family tree?'

'No. He's not fussy. Any old tree will do.'

A friend of mine plays the bugle and nearly got drowned the other day. He sounded the last post at a dog show.

A young girl wanted to give her dog a drink and was looking around for something to put the water in.

'Anyone seen the dog-bowl?' she asked the family in general.

'No,' replied her young brother, 'but I've seen him make some marvellous catches.'

A fisherman saw a bowler hat floating on the river, moving slowly against the current.

'Are you all right?' he shouted.

A hand came out of the water and raised the bowler hat. A voice said: 'Yes, thank you. I'm on a horse.'

A girl went for a donkey ride on the beach. But she couldn't get the donkey to move. So she got off it and asked the man in charge if *he* could make it go. The man walked round to the other side of the donkey, which suddenly took off and cantered away down the beach.

'What on earth did you do to it?' asked the girl.

'Oh, I just tickled his tummy, and off he went.'

'Well,' said the girl, 'now you'd better tickle mine. I've got to catch the bloody thing.'

Two flies in a teapot had a row. It all started when one flew off the handle.

Noel Coward was once taking one of his young godchildren for a walk when they saw two dogs mating.

'What are they doing, Uncle Noel?' asked the young boy.

7

'Oh,' said Coward without a moment's hesitation. 'One of the poor doggies has gone blind and the other is pushing him all the way to St Dunstan's.'

A farmer asked his young son to take a sow to the boar at the end of the village. On the way they met the vicar.
'Where are you going?' he asked the boy.
'I'm taking the sow to the boar, vicar.'
'Couldn't your father or brother do it, or can I help?'
'No, sorry vicar. It has to be the boar.'

A man once bought two budgerigars but was disappointed when after a few months there was no sign of any eggs. So he went to the shop where he had bought them and asked the proprietor whether there was any way of checking if they were in fact of different sexes, and if it was possible to tell which was which.
'Well yes,' he said. 'Get up at 3 a.m. one morning and creep down into the sitting-room. Lift up the cover of the cage and see if they are making love. If they are, the one on top will be the cock and I suggest that you tie a bit of white ribbon round his neck so that you will know him in the future.'
So the man did as suggested and sure enough there they were making love. So he got a bit of white ribbon and tied it round the neck of the bird on top. Next morning the vicar called and was shown into the sitting-room. The cock bird noticed his white collar and said: 'So he caught you at it too, did he?'

'Why are you looking so miserable?'
'I've just lost my dog.'
'Well, why not advertise for him in the paper?'
'It wouldn't be any good. He can't read.'

A blind man was walking along with his dog when it suddenly stopped and cocked its leg against the blind man's leg. He immediately felt his pocket and, bringing out a biscuit, offered it to the dog. A passer-by was amazed at what he saw.

8

'Considering what the dog has just done, that was a very kind act,' he told the blind man.

'No it wasn't,' said the blind man. 'I only did it to find out which end of the dog to kick.'

A vicar called on an old lady and much admired her talking parrot which he noticed had a red ribbon on its right leg and a blue one on its left.

'What are those for?' asked the vicar.

'If I pull the red ribbon he sings "Onward Christian Soldiers" and if I pull the blue one he sings "Abide With Me," she replied.

'But what happens if you pull both at the same time?' pressed the vicar.

'I fall off my perch, you silly old bugger,' chipped in the parrot.

A man was telling a friend about two elephants which were walking up Bond Street. One of the elephants told the other that he wanted to fart.

'Oh, you can't do it here,' said the other elephant, 'it will make far too much noise. You will have to go and do it in Hyde Park.'

The man then asked his friend: 'Have you heard it?'

'No,' said the friend.

'Well you would have done if you'd been in Hyde Park,' said the man.

A little old lady was sitting in front of the fire with her favourite tomcat on her knee. Suddenly there was a loud bang, a cloud of smoke, and a fairy appeared out of the fire.

'Little old lady,' she said. 'I can give you three wishes. What would you like?'

When she had recovered from the shock the little old lady said: 'First, I would like to be financially secure and live in a nice house for the rest of my life.'

The fairy waved her hand and the room was transformed into a luxurious drawing-room and on a table were sacks of gold. 'Next wish please,' she said.

'Please make me young and beautiful,' said the little old lady, and she was immediately turned into a glamorous blonde. 'For my third wish will you please turn my tomcat into a handsome young man.'

Immediately, standing before her was a fine specimen of manhood who stepped forward and took the 'old' lady's hand and kissed it.

'Now, aren't you sorry', he whispered, 'that you took me to the vet?'

A husband and wife went to the zoo, but the wife got too close to the bars of the cage containing an enormous gorilla. He seized her in his arms and started to kiss her.

'Help, help,' cried the wife to her husband. 'Do something quickly. He's trying to make love to me.'

'Well, tell him you've got a headache, like you always do to me,' replied the husband.

A circus was doing very badly. Audiences were dwindling and the proprietor was losing so much money that he realised that unless drastic action were taken he would have to close down. So he summoned all his staff and asked them to think up some publicity gimmick which would bring the crowds in. After a lot of discussion the elephant trainer came up with the following idea.

'My old elephant Jumbo is very obstinate and won't obey anyone but me. Why don't we offer a prize of £50 to anyone who can make him sit down in the ring. I guarantee he will just stand there, and refuse to budge unless *I* tell him.'

The proprietor thought this was a great stunt and he plastered the town with posters and leaflets announcing that on Saturday night there would be a sensational competition to see who could make Jumbo sit down. The prize was £50.

On Saturday the circus was packed out. The proprietor was delighted as he counted his takings. After the interval the ringmaster announced the competition and Jumbo was brought into the ring by his trainer. The audience were invited to step into the ring one by one and see if they could make the elephant sit down. A time limit of thirty minutes was set. There was a rush to have a go and people tried everything. They pulled the elephant's trunk, twisted his tail and shouted various words of command. But to no avail. Jumbo just stood there. After twenty-nine minutes the ringmaster announced

10

that there was only time for one more person to try. A small man stepped into the ring carrying a ladder. This he placed against the elephant's hind-quarters and up he climbed. When he got to the top he lifted the elephant's tail and gave him a tremendous kick in the arse. With a scream of pain the elephant immediately sat down. The small man climbed down his ladder, collected £50 from the ringmaster and left the ring to tumultuous applause.

Although he had had to fork out £50, the proprietor was delighted with the result – he had made a killing on the night. He was so pleased that he asked the trainer to think of another stunt for the following Saturday. The trainer said that he had thought of a certainty, which no one could possibly win. The task would be to make Jumbo first nod his head up and down and then shake it from side to side.

'He'll never do that for anyone,' said the trainer. 'He wouldn't even do it for me. Your £50 will be quite safe.'

So the same procedure was followed on the following Saturday and once again the circus tent was packed. The audience were told what they had to attempt and were invited to try their hand for half an hour. Hundreds of them came into the ring and tried everything to make Jumbo nod and shake his head. But he just stood there ignoring all their efforts and comments.

Finally, with one minute to go, the ringmaster announced that there was time for just one more person to try their luck. Once again the small man stepped into the ring with his ladder. This time he placed it against Jumbo's shoulder and climbed up. He took hold of Jumbo's ear and whispered into it.

'Do you remember what I did to you last Saturday?'

The elephant nodded his head up and down amidst roars of applause from the crowd. The small man then whispered again into Jumbo's ear.

'Do you want me to do it again?'

The elephant vigorously shook his head from side to side. The audience cheered and the small man stepped down the ladder and once again collected his £50 prize. A just reward for his remembering that simple adage: 'An elephant never forgets.'

A poor man and his donkey had been travelling all day and were both very tired. As night fell the man spotted a light at the end of a lane and approached what was obviously a farmhouse.

11

He knocked on the door and, when the farmer answered the man pleaded: 'Could you possibly give shelter for the night to myself and my donkey?'

The farmer was a kindly man and replied: 'Yes. There's a barn in the farmyard. It's full of straw and will be nice and warm. You are welcome to use it.'

The man thanked him, took the donkey into the barn and let him wander amongst the straw. The man settled down to sleep but, as he stretched his arms out he felt the figure of a naked woman asleep in the straw alongside him. It was pitch black so he couldn't see her but obviously she had a splendid figure. She stirred as he touched her and inevitably, after a short time, they made love. The man then went off to sleep until he was woken by a thin streak of light coming through the barn door. It was obviously time for him to get up and go. In the increased light he could just make out the shape of the woman lying a few feet away in the straw.

He shook her gently on the shoulder and said: 'I'm a poor man but I would be grateful if you will accept this 50p as a token of my appreciation of the pleasure which you gave me last night.'

The woman turned over and said: 'That is most kind of you and I'm very grateful. And what a contrast to your friend in the fur coat! He visited me three times and never even said thank you once.'

A woman had trained her parrot to give instructions to the various tradesmen when they called at the house. One day, when the coalman arrived, the parrot said: 'Ten sacks please.'

When he had made the delivery the coalman said to the parrot: 'You're a clever bird being able to talk like that.'

'Yes,' said the parrot. 'I can count too. Bring the other sack.'

An old lady had been a recluse all her life and hadn't seen much of what went on in the world. One day an elephant from a visiting circus escaped and broke into a small vegetable garden at the back of her house. She had never seen an elephant before and didn't know what it was, so she rang the local police.

'Officer,' she said. 'Please come round quickly to 1 Cavendish Street. There's a strange-looking animal in my garden and it's picking up my cabbages with its tail.'

'What's he doing with the cabbages?' asked the policeman.

'If I were to tell you, officer, you would arrest me for using rude words over the telephone.'

MONEY TALKS

Caller on the telephone: 'Can I speak to Mr Falkus, please?'
Secretary: 'No. I'm very sorry. He is not here this afternoon.'
Caller: 'Doesn't he work in the afternoons then?'
Secretary: 'Oh no. It's the mornings he doesn't work. He doesn't *come* in the afternoons.'

Manager to office boy: 'Thompson. You're late. You should have been here at nine-thirty.'
Thompson: 'Why, sir? What happened?'

'That's a very expensive fur coat for a struggling typist.'
'Yes. I decided to give up struggling.'

A man rushed into an office.
  'Do you believe in free speech?' he shouted to the man behind the desk.
  'Yes, of course I do,' said the businessman, slightly alarmed.
  'Right, let me use your telephone.'

Three bank clerks were always playing cards during business hours when the manager wasn't looking. One day he saw them playing, so he thought he would teach them a lesson and give them a fright. He rang the alarm bell three times, but despite this they went on playing. After a couple of minutes the barman from the pub opposite brought over three pints of beer.

Memo from Managing Director to Works Director
Tomorrow morning there will be a total eclipse of the sun at nine

o'clock. This is something which we cannot see happen every day, so let the workforce line up outside in their best clothes to watch it. To mark the occasion of this rare occurrence I will personally explain it to them. If it is raining we shall not be able to see it very well and in that case the workforce should assemble in the canteen.

Memo from Works Director to General Works Manager

By order of the managing director there will be a total eclipse of the sun at nine o'clock tomorrow morning. If it is raining we shall not be able to see it very well on site, in our best clothes. In that case the disappearance of the sun will be followed through in the canteen. This is something that we cannot see happen every day.

Memo from General Works Manager to Works Manager

By order of the managing director we shall follow through, in our best clothes, the disappearance of the sun in the canteen at nine o'clock tomorrow morning. The managing director will tell us whether it is going to rain. This is something which we cannot see happen every day.

Memo from Works Manager to Foreman

If it is raining in the canteen tomorrow morning, which is something that we cannot see happen every day, our managing director, in his best clothes, will disappear at nine o'clock.

Message from Foreman to Shop Floor:

Tomorrow morning at nine o'clock our managing director will disappear. It's a pity that we cannot see this happen every day.

A man reported to his insurance company that he had had a fire in his bedroom and his bed had been destroyed. The insurance company refused to pay the claim, saying that their client had obviously gone to bed drunk and set fire to his bed through his own carelessness. He replied that, in the first place he had been stone-cold sober, and secondly that the bed was already on fire when he got into it.

A FEW FOR THE ROAD, SOME FOR THE RAILS

'I call my new car Daisy.'
'Why?'
'Because some days it goes, some days it doesn't.'

'I've got a new car. It's a coup.'
'But surely you mean coupe? A coup's a thing you keep birds in.'
'So's my car!'

'I call my car Connie.'
'Why?'
'Short for constipation. It strains and strains and passes nothing.'

'My brother's car must be Jewish.'
'Why?'
'Well it's always breaking down and most days he vauxhall the way back to the garage.'

Why is a pedestrian crossing like a piece of lavatory paper?
You wait till all is safely passed. Then tear across the dotted line.

'Your car doesn't look too good. Have an accident?'
'No thanks. I've just had one.'

Country Mile – Distance between an empty petrol tank and the nearest filling station.

16

The best way to get rid of a noise in your car is to let her drive.

Motoring is like Russian roulette – you never know which driver is loaded.

In the early days people were flabbergasted when somebody drove at 15 mph – they still are.

The beauty of the old-fashioned blacksmith was that when you brought him your horse to be shod he didn't think of forty other things that ought to be done to it.

The best way to inspire courteous treatment by other motorists is to drive a police car.

Remember when it cost more to run a car than to park it?

When it comes to used cars, it's hard to drive a bargain.

Many a motorist whose eyes flit from limb to limb has hit a tree.

A reckless driver is one who passes you on the main road in spite of all you can do.

There are certain tips of value to the motorist on cold mornings. For example, before trying to start the car, check the bus timetable.

Motorist – one who keeps pedestrians in good running condition.

The best motorist drives with imagination; he imagines that his family is in the car.

Motorist – a person who after seeing a wreck drives carefully for several blocks.

Nothing depreciates a car faster than a neighbour buying a new one.

The greatest hazards on the roads are those under 21 driving over 65 and those over 65 driving under 21.

There were just as many reckless drivers seventy years ago – but in those days they drove something that had more sense than they did.

The trouble is that the car of tomorrow is being driven on the road of yesterday by the driver of today.

Some men have to shift for themselves – others get the instructions from the back seat.

You really wonder how the other half lives when you drive with some of them.

A red traffic light is the place where you catch up with a motorist who passed you at 60 mph ten blocks back.

Most road accidents are easily explained; the car is in gear and the driver's attention is in neutral.

A lady got on to a bus with a baby alligator in her arms. The conductor, somewhat surprised, asked: 'Are you taking him to the zoo, lady?'

'No,' she replied. 'We are going to the cinema. We went to the zoo yesterday.'

There was a dense fog in the city. The buses were crawling along. So a man walked behind his usual bus all the way home. He proudly told his wife what he had done.

'And, what's more,' he said, 'I've saved my usual 40p fare.'

'Why didn't you walk behind a taxi and save £3?' asked his wife.

Lady on bus: 'Do you stop at the Ritz, conductor?'
Conductor: 'No, madam. Not on my wages.'

A little girl used to bite her nails and to try to stop it her mother said to her: 'If you go on biting your nails, you'll get fat with a big tummy.'

The next day they got on a bus and her mother pointed to a large fat man of about 20 stone sitting opposite them. 'You'll get like him if you go on biting your nails,' she whispered.

At the next stop a blonde lady got on, obviously in an advanced stage of pregnancy. The little girl kept staring at her until the blonde couldn't stand it any more.

'Why are you looking at me like that? Do you know me?'

'No,' replied the little girl. 'I don't. But, I know what you've been up to.'

A man was out motoring with his wife who was a terrible back-seat driver. She always sat at the back and talked non-stop. Rather surprisingly he had not heard a single word from her for about a minute when a policeman on a motorbike roared up alongside him and signalled to him to stop.

'Excuse me, sir,' said the policeman. 'Do you realise the back door of your car is open and a lady fell out about half a mile back?'

'Thank God for that,' said the motorist. 'It must be my wife. I thought I had gone deaf.'

A man was standing in a bus queue immediately behind a gorgeous blonde. She had on one of those tight dresses fitting very closely round her knees. It also had a row of buttons down the back. When the bus came along the blonde tried to get on. But her dress was so tight round her knees that she couldn't get up on the step. So she put her hand behind her back, undid a bottom button and tried again, without success. She did this several times, each time undoing another button.

The conductor was getting a bit impatient, so the young man said: 'Allow me to help,' and lifted her up on to the step of the bus.

As it set off she turned to the young man and said: 'Thank you so much for your kindness in helping me. You've no idea how embarrassing it was undoing all those buttons in public.'

'You're telling me,' said the young man. 'They weren't yours.'

A well-dressed man driving a brand-new Rolls-Royce drew up at a village petrol pump, deep in the countryside. It was one of those old-fashioned pumps where the attendant had to pump by hand.
Attendant: 'Do you live round here?'
Man in Rolls: 'No.'
Attendant: 'On holiday?'
Man in Rolls: 'No.'
Attendant: 'Have you got a job here?'
Man in Rolls: 'No.'
Attendant: 'What are you then? What do you do?'
Man in Rolls: 'Well, actually, I work for Cunard.'
Attendant: 'So do I. Fourteen hours a day. But *I* can't afford a Rolls.'

A man ran out of petrol in the middle of a village opposite the local pub. He asked a man sitting outside with a pint in his hand whether he would be so kind as to push his car for him up to the petrol pump 400 yards away. Rather reluctantly the man agreed and with great difficulty pushed the car up the village street. By the time he reached the pump he was hopelessly out of breath. The driver, who had sat in the car in order to steer, asked for £10 worth of petrol. When the tank was full, he gave the attendant a £10 note and then searched in his pockets for some small change with which to tip the man who had pushed him.

Finding that he had no money left, he unwound his car window and said to the pusher: 'I'm sorry, I've spent all my money on the petrol, so I have none to give you. Do you smoke, by any chance?'

20

The pusher replied: 'Yes, sir, I do.'

The driver countered: 'Well, if I were you I'd give it up. You look half-knackered,' and so saying, wound up his window and drove off.

A motorist got lost on the A3 just after leaving Guildford. He stopped and addressed a man waiting at a bus-stop.

'Excuse me, do you know the Hog's Back?'

'No,' replied the man. 'I didn't know that he'd been away.'

A man was motoring along a main road when he saw a very attractive blonde by the side of the road, thumbing a lift. So he stopped and asked her to get into his car. As they were going along, in order to make conversation he asked her what she did for a living.

'Oh, I'm a witch,' she replied casually.

The motorist was naturally very surprised.

'I don't believe it,' he said. 'Can you prove it?'

Saying nothing the blonde put her hand on his knee and then started to run her fingers up the inside of his thigh – and he immediately turned into a lay-by.

A man was belting up a road at 80 mph when just ahead of him a tractor with two men on it slowly came out of a gate and on to the road. Realising that if he went straight on he would hit the tractor, he swung violently to the left and shot through the gate into the field from which the tractor had just come. He bumped along the field parallel to the road for a few yards and then noticed a gap in the hedge. So he drove through it back on to the road and continued his journey at speed as if nothing had happened.

'You know, George,' said one of the men on the tractor to the other, 'we only just got out of that field in time.'

A Mini broke down and its owner was standing disconsolately by the side of the road. A very posh new Jaguar drew up and its driver asked if he could help.

The Mini owner said he did not know what was wrong, so the man in the Jaguar said: 'OK, I'll give you a tow. I've got a very thin nylon

21

rope in my boot. I'll go along slowly, but if anything is wrong, blow your horn like mad.'

So they set off slowly and were cruising along at a steady 30 mph. Suddenly a big red Mercedes passed them at a great speed. This nettled the Jaguar driver, who thought that, for the sake of Queen and country, he should show that British was best. So, forgetting he had the Mini in tow, he set off in pursuit. He soon reached 100 mph and was gaining on the Mercedes. The poor man in the Mini wondered what on earth was happening. Remembering what he had been told he started to hoot like mad as his Mini was swaying and jumping about all over the place.

As he did so they passed a police car in a lay-by, whose driver, in amazement, got on to the radio to speak to a colleague further up the road.

'There's a crazy race going on. A Mercedes going about 100 mph is just about to be passed by a Jaguar. And, believe it or not, right up behind the Jaguar, nearly touching his rear bumper, is a Mini. Its driver looks terrified but is sounding his horn trying to pass them both.'

A wife had just been given a brand-new Volkswagen for her birthday. She immediately went out for a drive as it was the first time she had ever seen a car like it. After about ten minutes it broke down and, try as she could on the self-starter, she could not get the engine to go. Although she knew nothing about cars she got out and lifted up the bonnet to see if she could see anything wrong. To her horror there was no engine there. At that moment, another lady came towards her also in another brand-new Volkswagen, and stopped to ask if she could help.

'Thank you so much,' said the first lady, 'but I don't really think you can. You see my engine has fallen out.'

'Oh, but I *can* help you then,' said the second lady. 'I happened to open my boot this morning and I found that I had a spare engine in it.'

A young girl, nursing a baby, was sitting in a train and the man in the seat opposite her kept staring at the baby. After about ten minutes, the girl got a bit fed up and said to the man: 'What on earth are you staring at my baby for?'

The man replied that he'd rather not say, but kept on staring from time to time. Finally the girl exploded.

'Look, you *must* tell me the reason for your extraordinary behaviour, or I shall call the guard.'

'Well,' said the man, 'if you really insist on knowing, it's because your baby is the ugliest I have ever seen.'

On hearing this the girl burst into tears and took the baby out into the corridor of the train. She was standing there, crying her eyes out, when a man came past and, seeing the state she was in, asked what was the matter. Through her sobs the girl explained that she had just been grossly insulted by a man in her compartment.

'Cheer up,' said the passer-by. 'I'm going along to the restaurant car, and before I have my meal I'll bring you back a cup of tea.'

He returned about five minutes later. 'Here's your cup of tea,' he said sympathetically. 'I hope it will do you good. And, what's more, I've brought a banana for the monkey.'

A man was travelling in the bottom berth of a second-class sleeper on the Glasgow to London night train. The top berth was unoccupied. After the train had stopped at Carlisle, the steward knocked on his door.

'Excuse me, sir, sorry to wake you. But I have a young lady here who cannot find a seat or a sleeping berth. Would you object if she used the top bunk? Otherwise she will have to stand up all the night.'

'Certainly, she can come in,' said the man sleepily.

He looked up to see a smashing blonde, who clambered up to the top bunk and, after a few words of gratitude, appeared to settle down for the night.

But after a quarter of an hour or so she put her head over the edge and whispered: 'Are you awake? If so, I'm absolutely freezing up here. Could you go and ask the steward for another blanket, please?'

After a pause the man replied: 'I've got a far better idea. For the rest of the journey, why don't we pretend that we are a married couple?'

'Oh, yes,' said the blonde, 'that would be nice,' and swung her legs over the top bunk.

'Right,' said the man. 'Let's start as we are going to continue. *You* go and fetch the bloody blanket.'

Four men were travelling in the Flying Scotsman on its non-stop journey to Edinburgh. Each sat in a corner reading his newspaper and not a word passed between them.

When they passed through Hitchin – about 32 miles – one of the men put down *The Times* which he was reading and said: 'Look, we've got about another 360 miles to go. Let's introduce ourselves and talk. The journey will go ever so much more pleasantly. I'll start by telling you that I'm a brigadier, I'm married, I have one son who is a banker.'

The man sitting opposite him put down his *Times* and said: 'What an amazing coincidence. I'm also a brigadier. I'm also married and have one son who is a schoolmaster.'

The man in the third corner looked amazed. 'This really is extraordinary,' he said, as he put down his *Times*. 'I'm a brigadier, I'm married and I have a son who is a lawyer.'

They all looked at the fourth man who was reading the *Daily Mirror*, but he shook his head and murmured that he would rather not join in. So the other three chatted among themselves and were obviously enjoying each other's company.

After half an hour or so they turned to the fourth man again and one of them said: 'Do join in with us. The journey is going so much more quickly now that we all know each other.'

But the man shook his head vehemently.

'Oh, come on,' they all said. 'Do change your mind.'

'All right,' he said, putting down the *Daily Mirror*. 'Have it your own way. I am a regimental sergeant-major. I am *not* married, I have three sons, and they are all brigadiers.'

A smartly dressed salesman had been standing all day on the Rolls-Royce stand at the Motor Show. A man approached him and asked if the salesman knew the way to the nearest lavatory.

'Certainly,' said the salesman, 'I'll take you there myself.'

'That's very kind of you,' said the man. 'There's really no need to take so much trouble.'

'Don't mention it, it's a pleasure. Yours is the first genuine enquiry I have had all day,' replied the salesman.

A woman went to the Motor Show and approached one of the stands.

A sleek, good-looking young salesman spotted her and said: 'Do you want a baby Austin?'

'How did you know my name was Austin? But, anyway, I don't want one. My husband has just bought a new Dodge.'

A lady carrying a small dog tried to board a bus.

'Sorry, madam,' said the conductor. 'No dogs allowed on the bus.'

The lady was angry and shouted: 'Oh, stuff your bus.'

'Well, madam,' shouted back the conductor, 'if you can do the same with your dog, you can come on the bus.'

A man standing behind a young lady on a moving staircase at Piccadilly Circus tube station noticed that one of her breasts was hanging out of her dress. She didn't seem aware of it, so he bravely touched her on the shoulder and told her about it.

'Oh, thank goodness you've told me. I must have left the baby on the train,' she said.

An old lady was finding it very difficult to get on to a bus. But the Sikh conductor, who was wearing his turban, gave her a hand and helped her to a seat.

'That was very kind of you,' she said. 'And I do hope your head is better in the morning.'

An enormously fat lady got on to a bus which was full, with standing room only. As she hung on to a strap she glared round the bus at the passengers, most of whom were men.

'Isn't anyone going to offer me a seat?'

At this, a tiny man got up and said meekly: 'I'm willing to make a small contribution.'

A man was driving his large Bentley down a narrow country lane. As he approached a corner a lady in a Mini came slowly round and had to go up on to the grass verge to avoid the Bentley. She wound down her window and shouted out: 'Pig.'

The driver of the Bentley was annoyed at this and, unwinding *his* window, shouted back: 'Silly old bitch.'

25

He then drove slowly forward and, as he went round the corner, he saw a large pig squatting in the middle of the lane.

A man driving past a farmyard accidently ran over a cockerel. He went up to the farmhouse and knocked on the door.

'I'm terribly sorry,' he told the farmer's wife. 'I've just run over your cockerel and I would like to replace him.'

'Please yourself,' she said. 'The hens are round the back.'

A lorry driver was sitting eating his lunch in a roadside cafe when about ten Hell's Angels came barging in. They took the place over, swaggering about, shouting and swearing. Then they started to take the mickey out of the lorry driver. When he didn't react they poured coffee all over him and upset his plate of eggs and beans. He just sat there without saying a word or offering any resistance. Finally, near to tears, he got up, paid the girl behind the counter and left the cafe.

One of the Hell's Angels turned to the girl and said: 'Not much of a man, was he?'

'No,' she said, looking out of the window. 'And he's not much of a driver either. He's just backed his lorry into ten motorbikes.'

A driver rang the police. 'Come at once, please. Someone has stolen my steering wheel and column, and the clutch, brake and accelerator pedals. Please hurry.'

He went back to his car again, and opened the door. He immediately rushed back into his house and rang the police again.

'Cancel that last call of mine, please. I find that I was sitting in the back seat.'

A motorist who had broken down stopped a car approaching him and went up to the driver's window.

'I've got engine trouble. Are you by any chance an expert on engines?'

'No,' said the driver. 'I'm not. I'm a chiropodist. But I can always give you a to(e)w.'

A police car patrolman flagged down a motorist during a check for some stolen property. The conversation went as follows:

'What's your name?'
'Santall.'
'What's the make of your car?'
'Vauxhall.'
'Where have you come from?'
'Walsall.'
'Where are you going?'
'Luggershall.'
'What's in the boot of your car?'
'Nothing.'

MEDICINE MEN

A man went into a chemist's shop and asked for a tin of talcum powder.

'Certainly sir,' said the chemist, stepping out from behind the counter.

'Please walk this way.'

'If I could walk that way,' replied the man, 'I wouldn't need the talcum powder.'

A young lady had one of those tiny Chihuahua dogs. It became ill, and all its hair started falling out. So she left it at home and went to the local chemist.

'Have you got something for falling hair, please?' she asked.

'Yes, certainly madam,' replied the chemist, reaching up to take a bottle off a shelf. 'Just rub this into your head three times a day and you should soon be better. But there must be no pressure on your head, so don't wear a hat for a fortnight.'

'Oh,' said the girl, 'it's not for *my* head. It's for my Chihuahua.'

'In that case, madam,' said the chemist, 'I'd recommend you not to ride a bike for a week.'

A young man was going to take a girl to a dance. On the way to pick her up at her home, he stopped at a chemist's just before closing time.

'Sorry to trouble you so late, but could I please have some contraceptives? I need them badly for tonight.'

He bought some and, as he left, the chemist closed the shop for the night. The young man thought he would have a drink at a pub to give him more confidence, and after that he went to the girl's home.

She opened the door and said: 'Oh, hello. I'm just ready. But while I'm doing my nails perhaps you'd like to go into the sitting-room to meet my father who has just come home.'

The young man went into the room, rather nervous at the prospect of meeting the girl's father. He was sitting in a chair reading the evening paper. When he put the paper down the young man nearly fainted. It was the chemist!

At a party a man pulled his handkerchief out of his coat pocket and about ten packets of aspirin spilled out on to the floor.

'What on earth have you got all those for?' asked a friend.

'Oh,' he replied, 'I wanted to buy something from a chemist but, at each shop I went into there was a lady behind the counter.'

A man went into a chemist and asked for some rat poison.

'I'm sorry, we don't stock it,' said the assistant. 'Why not try Boots?'

'I want to poison them, not kick them to death,' replied the man.

'Why don't they sell Lucozade in Boots?'
'Because it runs through the lace-holes.'

'Can I have a tablet of soap please?'
'Certainly, madam. Would you like it scented?'
'No thank you. I'll take it with me.'

A husband was pacing up and down in a hospital waiting-room for the arrival of his first child. At 9.15 p.m. a nurse rushed up to him and said: 'Many congratulations. You're the proud father of a lovely-looking baby girl.'

'How amazing,' said the man. That's nine months to the minute since our honeymoon first night.'

A quarter of an hour later the nurse came back. 'Many more congratulations. You've now got a baby boy.'

The husband continued pacing up and down and, as the clock

read 9.45 p.m., the nurse returned yet again. She was very excited.

'It's triplets – another boy. Well done.'

The husband thanked her and put on his coat and hat.

'Where are you going?' asked the nurse. 'Don't you want to wait and see your wife?'

'No,' said the husband. 'I'm going out for a drink. There's nothing more due till 11.15 p.m.'

A man had just learned that his wife had presented him with quins. He was justifiably proud.

'I should be,' he said. 'I must have a pretty good chimney,'

'Well,' said the nurse who had brought the good news, 'I should get it swept if I were you. All five are black.'

A lady who had just had triplets was asked by her nurse what she was going to call them.

'John, James and Tat,' was her reply. 'Because I have no tit for Tat.'

Charlie Harris, the Nottinghamshire cricketer, once dislocated his shoulder and was sent to hospital. There they tried to put the shoulder back without giving him an anaesthetic. It was so painful that Charlie shouted and screamed.

'Mr Harris,' said one of the nurses, 'do try to be brave. There is a lady having a baby down the corridor and she is not making half the fuss that you are.'

'No,' said Charlie, 'but they are not trying to put it back.'

A lecturer in a teaching hospital was trying to demonstrate the danger of too much drink. To prove his point he placed a live worm in a glass of water and another live worm in a glass of whisky. At the end of his lecture he turned to the two glasses. The worm in the water was wriggling about strongly but the worm in the whisky was still, and obviously stone dead.

The lecturer turned to his audience of medical students and said: 'What is the lesson to be learned from my demonstration?'

A voice from the back quickly replied: 'If you don't want to get worms, drink whisky.'

A man woke up after an operation and through a mist saw a figure standing by his bed.

'Was my operation a success, doctor?' he whispered.

'I don't know, old chap,' said the figure. 'I'm St Peter.'

A man who had had a hernia operation was recommended to convalesce by the sea for a week. So, he went to a Truss House Hotel in Hernia Bay where he was given a rupturous reception.

A woman went to a doctor with a bad cough. After he had examined her he said: 'Do you ever get a tickle in the morning?'

'Well, I used to,' replied the woman, 'but not now. They've changed the milkman.'

A mother took her 10 year-old son to the doctor.

'Doctor,' she said. 'I am very worried. My son thinks he's a hen, and can't stop clucking.'

'How long has this been going on?' asked the doctor.

'Oh about five years,' replied the mother.

'Then why on earth didn't you bring him to me before this?'

'Well, candidly, doctor, we needed the eggs.'

A small boy swallowed a £1 note. His mother rang up the doctor in a panic.

'What shall I do, doctor?'

'Oh,' said the doctor, 'give him some pills and give me a ring in two days' time if there is no change.'

A very good golfer gradually began to lose his ability to drive the ball a long way. He had consistently been able to hit at least 250 yards but over a few months his drives became shorter and shorter. It became so bad that he could hardly reach 120 yards. So, very worried, he visited his doctor and told him his trouble.

The doctor examined him thoroughly and then said: 'Put your clothes on and I've got two bits of news for you, one good and the other bad.'

The golfer dressed hurriedly and said: 'Right. Let's have the bad news first.'

'Well,' said the doctor, 'I'm sorry to tell you, but you are gradually changing into a woman.'

The golfer was visibly shocked. 'Quick tell me the good news.'

'From now on,' said the doctor, 'you'll be able to drive off the ladies tees.'

A doctor examined a man and then told him he had two bits of news for him, bad and good. 'The bad news is that you've turned into a poof. The good news is that I love you.'

A man went to the doctor because he could not stop coughing. The doctor gave him a large dose of cascara. When the man asked if it would cure the cause of the cough, he replied: 'No. But you won't dare to cough.'

A nun visited a doctor with a violent attack of hiccups. The doctor told her she was pregnant. His assistant asked him if she really was. 'No,' said the doctor. 'But the shock stopped her hiccups.'

A man was worried about his sex life.

'How often should I have sex, doctor?' he asked.

'Infrequently,' said the doctor.

'Is that one word or two?' asked the man.

A man broke his finger which his doctor put into a splint.

'Will I be able to play the guitar when it's better?' he asked the doctor.

'Yes, of course you will,' the doctor replied.

'Funny,' said the man, 'I've never been able to play it before.'

A woman was sitting nervously in the dentist's chair waiting to have a tooth stopped. The dentist approached her with the drill and asked her to open her mouth.

Suddenly, he stopped and said: 'Excuse, me madam. Do you realise that your right hand is gripping me in a very painful place?'

'Yes,' said the woman, 'I do. We're not going to hurt each other, are we?'

An attractive young girl suddenly felt ill in the middle of the night. Her father rang the doctor and asked him to come as soon as possible. When the doctor arrived he rushed up the stairs and the father showed him into his daughter's bedroom. The father then went downstairs where he and his wife had a cup of tea. After about half an hour they wondered what was wrong with their daughter, so anxiously went and listened outside her bedroom door. Hearing voices, the father listened at the keyhole.

He heard his daughter pleading: 'Kiss me, doctor, kiss me.'

'I'm sorry, young lady, I can't do that,' replied the doctor. 'It would be completely unethical. Strictly speaking, I shouldn't even be in bed with you.'

A man went to the doctor's with very bad laryngitis. The receptionist, who was a lovely girl, opened the door.

'Is the doctor here?' he whispered hoarsely.

'No,' she replied in a whisper, 'come in.'

A girl told her doctor that she had a very unusual complaint.

'Every time I sneeze, I get an uncontrollable urge to make love with someone.'

'How often do you sneeze?' he asked.

'Oh, quite frequently,' she replied.

'And how long have you had this complaint?'

'Oh, about six months,' said the girl.

'Six months,' exclaimed the doctor. 'Why haven't you been to see me before? What have you been doing about it?

'Taking snuff,' was the reply.

A man had a bad attack of that very painful 'universal complaint'. The doctor examined his backside and said he would like to try out a new cure he had just heard about from a gipsy. The man agreed and the doctor put a lot of tea-leaves in the appropriate place, saying it would take about two weeks to effect a cure. But after a week the pain was still so bad that the man became impatient and decided to go to a more orthodox doctor.

He told him what was wrong and after the examination the doctor said: 'Well, I'm afraid the only thing I can do for you is to give you some ointment. But, I'll tell you something interesting. I can see a tall dark stranger and you are going on a long journey with a beautiful lady.'

A man with a bad inferiority complex went to see his doctor.
'Doctor, please help. Nobody ever notices me.'
The doctor said: 'Next patient, please.'

Doctor: 'I'm afraid I can't diagnose your complaint. I think it must be drink.'
Patient: 'All right then, I'll come back when you are sober.'

An absent-minded man went to see a psychiatrist.
'My trouble is,' he said, 'that I keep forgetting things.'
'How long has this been going on?' asked the psychiatrist.
'How long has *what* been going on?' said the man.

A doctor had just finished examining his lady patient.
'I've got some good news for you, Mrs Green.'
'Miss Green, doctor,' said the patient.
'In that case, I've got some *bad* news for you. You are going to have a baby.'

A young wife suspected that she was pregnant, so went to see her doctor. He examined her and told her that it was only wind. Shortly afterwards he left for the USA to go on an exchange with an

American doctor. He returned to his practice after the year was up, and one day saw the young wife pushing a double pram with twins in it.

'Ah,' he said, 'I see you've had twins since I've been away.'

'No, doctor,' said the young wife. 'Just two farts with bonnets on.'

A man went to see his doctor because his hands kept shaking.

'Do you drink much?' asked the doctor.

'No,' said the man. 'I spill most of it.'

A prostitute felt ill so went to see her doctor, who examined her and said: 'There's nothing much wrong with you. I'll give you some pills and then take it easy for a bit. A week or two on your feet and we'll soon have you on your back again.'

A man went to see a doctor in a great panic.

'Doctor, please examine me at once. I think I'm going to have a baby.'

The doctor examined him and said: 'By God. You're right. This will cause a tremendous sensation when I tell my colleagues in Harley Street.'

'It will back home in Laburnam Crescent too,' said the man. 'I'm not even married.'

After examining a patient, the doctor reached for the pen in his breast pocket and brought out a suppository. 'Oh, damn,' he said. 'Some ass has got my pen.'

A Chinese man rang his dentist for an appointment.

'What time you fix, please?'

'Two-thirty all right?' asked the dentist.

'Tooth hurty all right, but what time can you fix?'

'I reckon old Bill will be in hospital for some time yet.'

'Pretty ill, eh?'

'No, pretty nurse.'

35

There was a long queue in the doctor's waiting-room. Suddenly the door from the street opened and an Indian came in and immediately jumped the queue. Naturally everyone was indignant and tried to stop him as he fought his way along.

'What do you think you're doing?' asked a big man at the head of the queue. 'Wait your turn like we've all been doing for the last hour.'

'Yes,' gasped the Indian. 'I'm sorry, I'm late. I'm the doctor.'

A lady patient rang up her doctor one day. He was a good doctor, but couldn't resist making facetious jokes.

'Can you help me, doctor? I can't get to sleep at nights,' she asked on the telephone. She didn't appreciate the answer she got.

'Why not try lying on the edge of the bed. You'll soon drop off.'

The same doctor was visited by another patient who complained that he snored so loudly that he even kept himself awake.

'I suggest that you try sleeping in another room,' said the doctor unhelpfully.

'Doctor, doctor. My little Willie has just swallowed a teaspoon. Please come at once.'

'Very well, madam. I'll be right round. But meanwhile, tell him to sit still and not to stir.'

Doctor: 'What's the matter with you?'
Patient: 'I keep thinking I'm a pack of cards.'
Doctor: 'Well, stop shuffling about and I'll deal with you in a minute.'

Patient: 'I keep thinking I'm a pair of curtains.'
Doctor: 'Come, come. Pull yourself together.'

Patient: 'I feel like a billiard ball.'
Doctor: 'Go to the end of the cue.'

36

Patient: 'Doctor, why does matron keep telling me that I've got to try to cheer you up?'
Doctor: 'Because I'm worried to death about you.'

Patient: 'I keep thinking I'm a bell.'
Doctor: 'Well, take these pills and if you're no better in two days give me a ring.'

A doctor was examining a male patient who was very fat.

'If I saw a stomach like that on a woman I would say that she was pregnant,' said the doctor.

'You're quite right, doctor. It *was* and she *is*,' said the patient.

I AM THE VICAR

Two bishops were in London to attend a week's synod at Church House. They were having tea and crumpets in front of the fire at the Athenaeum, discussing how they were going to deal with the subject of the next day's conference. It was an awkward topic for a bishop – pre-marital sex.

'For instance,' said one bishop, 'I never slept with my wife before I married her. Did you?'

'I can't remember,' said the other bishop, 'what was her maiden name?'

A bishop had a bad reputation in his diocese for preaching long and very boring sermons. His reputation spread rapidly, because each Sunday he used to visit a different parish to preach. One day he arrived at five to eleven at a small country church and was welcomed by the vicar who was looking a bit flustered. He led the bishop into the church and, to the bishop's surprise and annoyance, there were only three people in the congregation.

'Didn't you warn them that I was coming?' he asked the vicar angrily.

'I certainly did not, bishop,' replied the vicar. 'But, I shall do my very best to find out who did!'

A bishop was presenting the prizes at a school. He got tired of saying the same words of congratulation to each recipient. So, when a pretty blonde girl came up to receive her prize he thought he would try something different.

'What are you going to do when you leave school, my dear?' he asked.

'Well, bishop,' she replied, blushing. 'I was going home for tea with my mother. But, I could cancel that.'

A young vicar went to a new parish and soon created a great impression with the parishioners with his down-to-earth sermons. After he had been there for about a month he met an elderly lady in the village street.

'Oh, vicar,' she said. 'We are all so glad that you are here. Until you came we didn't know what real sin was.'

A bishop was doing a crossword puzzle in a crowded railway carriage. After filling in some clues, he suddenly looked very puzzled.

After a minute or so he said out loud: 'Can anyone help me? I want a four-letter word ending in **-UNT** with female connections.'

After a short pause a young man suggested: 'What about **AUNT**, sir?'

'Ah, thank you so much,' replied the bishop. 'I thought I must be wrong. Anyone got a rubber?'

A parishioner asked her local vicar: 'Vicar, do you know? Did St Paul ever get a reply to that remarkably long letter to the Corinthians?'

A bishop was sitting in the Athenaeum and had just ordered a whisky and soda. While waiting for it he fell asleep. The club steward bought the whisky and poured soda into it from a siphon, making quite a splash. Without opening his eyes the bishop said: 'Is that you out of bed again, Milly?'

A vicar thought that a spot of advertising for his church would not do any harm. So, he put up a big poster with the slogan: 'If you are tired of sin, please step inside.'

The next day, he saw scribbled underneath it: 'But if you are not, telephone St John's Wood 29591.'

A young man about to be married asked his vicar whether he had any strong objections to sex before the marriage.

After a moment's hesitation, the vicar replied: 'No, not really. So long as it doesn't keep the wedding guests waiting.'

A parishioner was having supper at the vicarage and, when the vicar poured out the wine, he missed her out.
'Could I have some wine please, vicar?' she asked.
'Oh, I'm sorry – I thought you were a member of the Temperance League,' he explained.
'No, no, vicar. I'm a member of the Purity League.'
'Ah,' he said. 'I knew there was something you didn't do.'

A bishop was visiting a primary school.
'I'll give a penny to the boy or girl who tells me who I am,' he proclaimed.
A small boy said: 'Please sir, you are God.'
'No, I am not,' said the bishop. 'But, here's twopence.'

In pre-war days a vicar was driving his bishop round the parish in a pony cart. As they were bowling along the village street the pony let out a rude noise.
'Sorry about that, bishop,' said the vicar slightly embarrassed.
'Not to worry,' said the bishop. 'If you hadn't mentioned it I'd have thought it was the pony.'

One of our archbishops sailed on the *Queen Elizabeth* on his first visit to America. On arrival at New York he was surrounded by reporters. The first question was from a tough Brooklyn reporter who asked the archbishop if he intended to visit any of New York's infamous striptease clubs.
The archbishop thought carefully before answering. '*Are* there any striptease clubs in New York?'
The next day's headlines in the press read: 'Archbishop's first question: "Are there any striptease clubs in New York." '

A man used to go to the same barber regularly once a fortnight. He was an excellent barber, but had the annoying habit of belittling anything his customer said. One fortnight the customer said he had bought a new car.

'What sort?' asked the barber.

'A Ford,' said the customer.

'Oh,' said the barber. 'Never get a Ford. Get any other car, but *not* a Ford.'

The following fortnight the customer was saying that he had just bought a new fridge and mentioned the name.

Immediately the barber said: 'You've bought one of those? They always break down. Any other make but *not* that.'

The following fortnight the customer said he was going on holiday to Rome.

'Why choose Rome?' asked the barber.

'Well,' said the customer. 'It is my ambition to see the Pope and, if possible, to be spoken to by him.'

'You're crazy to go to Rome. Anywhere else, but *not* Rome. And, anyway, I bet you £50 that the Pope doesn't talk to you.'

The customer was so fed up that he rashly accepted the challenge. A month later he went to the barber, who promptly asked him how he had got on in Rome and reminded him of the £50 bet.

'Oh no,' said the customer. 'You owe *me* £50. The Pope *did* speak to me.'

The barber was incredulous. 'How and where did it happen.' he asked.

'Well,' said the customer. 'I was wandering around St Peter's Square one day hoping to catch sight of the Pope when, to my surprise and delight, I saw him walking towards me. I was even more surprised when he stopped and addressed a few words to me.'

'Go on. What did he say?' asked the barber in disbelief.

'Oh, he just said quietly to me: "Do tell me. Where on earth did you get that terrible haircut?" ' (Collapse of barber.)

A rich English Roman Catholic had one wish. He wanted to meet the Pope personally and was prepared to spend as long as necessary in Rome until he did so. So everyday he joined the crowds in St Peter's Square and occasionally saw the Pope on his balcony. But that was the nearest he ever got. He was beginning to despair when one day he went to the British Embassy to sign the ambassador's book. A

41

young attaché saw him sign it and asked if he would like a ticket for a garden party which the Pope was giving in the Vatican the next day. The only snag was that he would have to wear full morning dress. The man was delighted and said the clothes were no problem. So he was given a ticket, went off to the equivalent of Moss Bros and hired himself some morning clothes.

The next day he went to the Vatican dressed in his morning suit and top hat. He waited in a line of guests waiting for the Pope to appear. The guests were drawn up in two lines facing each other, so that the Pope could walk down one line and then turn and go back along the other line. He appeared to great applause. The Englishman was standing there hopefully as the Pope proceeded down the line. But he spoke to nobody, just waved his hands in a sort of blessing and proceeded to the end of the line.

There, to the surprise of the Englishman, stood a dirty looking tramp in the most dreadful old clothes – a real contrast to the immaculately dressed throng. The Englishman was even more surprised when he saw the Pope put his hands on the tramp's shoulders and whisper something in his ear. The Englishman thought quickly to himself: Obviously the Pope will only talk to someone who is poor, down and out and needing special words of comfort.

So he quickly rushed up the line, got hold of the tramp and asked him if he would change clothes with him for a thousand lire. The tramp couldn't believe his ears and instantly agreed. So they went behind a large bush and quickly exchanged clothes. Dressed now as the tramp, the Englishman just had time to rush to the end of the second line, down which the Pope was proceeding. His heart beat faster as the Pope came nearer and then, to his utter joy, the Pope approached him and put both his hands on his shoulders – just as he had done to the tramp. The Englishman couldn't believe it. The Pope was going to talk to him. His wish had come true. And here it was, the Pope was whispering in his ear....

'I thought that just now I had told you to bugger off!'

A group of visitors was being shown round a monastery. When they came to the kitchens, they saw a monk preparing a meal of fish and chips. A clever dick went up to the monk and asked: 'Are you the chipmonk?'

'No,' was the reply. 'I'm the head friar.'

A vicar noticed that one of his oldest and most regular attendants at church always bowed her head whenever the vicar mentioned Satan or the Devil. He asked her one day why she did it.

'Because, vicar, I've always been taught that politeness costs nothing.'

A new vicar thought he would try to reform a local girl who was said to be very free with her favours. So he knocked on her front door, which was ajar.

'Come in,' said a voice. 'My door is always open.'

The vicar stepped inside and there, lying on a sofa stark naked, was a beautiful blonde. He was horrified.

'Young lady,' he said, 'I've heard all about you. You should be on your knees.'

'Oh well,' she said, 'if it's kinky it's extra.'

A clergyman prided himself on his spontaneity and told a friend that he could preach a sermon on any subject at a moment's notice. His friend challenged him to do so on the following Sunday and said he would put a piece of paper with the required subject in the pulpit, just before the service.

When the time for the sermon came the clergyman mounted the pulpit and there found the promised slip of paper. On it was written just one word: 'Constipation.' The clergyman paused for a moment and then said: 'My text is taken from the Book of Exodus, Chapter 34. "And Moses took the tablets and went up into the mountain".'

Moses spent several days and nights in the mountain 'negotiating' with God about the Commandments. One morning he came rushing down the mountain and summoned the multitude.

'Gather round,' he cried. 'I've got two bits of news about the Commandments. One good, one bad. The good news is that we have got them down to ten.'

There were loud cheers from the multitude.

'What about the bad news, then, Moses?' they shouted.

'Well,' he said, 'the bad news is that adultery is in!'

A vicar lost his bicycle and suspected that someone must have stolen it. So he told the verger that on the next Sunday when he was reading out the Ten Commandments he would pause significantly after number eight 'Thou shalt not steal.' He asked the verger to watch the congregation carefully and see whether he could spot anyone looking guilty.

After the service the verger said to the vicar: 'You never paused as you said you would after the eighth commandment.'

'No,' said the vicar. 'I didn't. Because, when I read out the seventh commandment I remembered where I had left my bicycle.'

Two Americans visiting Canterbury were having coffee in a cafe. Sitting at a table nearby was a distinguished-looking, grey-haired man. One of the Americans said it looked just like the Archbishop of Canterbury and they began to argue about it. So they eventually decided to have a bet and one of them got up and went over to the grey-haired man's table to ask him whether he *was* the archbishop. He returned fairly quickly to their table and his companion asked him what the man had said.

'He told me to bugger off and mind my own bloody business.'

'Oh, what a pity,' said the second American. 'Now we shall never know whether he was the archbishop or not.'

A vicar thought that it was time to give his congregation a strong warning of the punishment that lay ahead for sinners.

'I warn you,' he thundered, 'that for those of you sinners who do not repent, there will be weeping and gnashing of teeth.'

At this point an old lady stood up. 'Please, sir,' she said. 'What will happen to me? I have no teeth.'

'Madam,' said the vicar, nothing daunted, 'teeth will be provided.'

A vicar was giving his Christmas sermon.

'It is a time of great joy for all God's two-legged creatures,' he proclaimed piously.

A voice at the back of the congregation shouted out: 'Try telling that to a turkey.'

Another vicar received a Christmas present of a bottle of cherry brandy from a parishioner. He decided to acknowledge the kind gift at his next service. So, when he came to the notices, he said: 'I would like to thank Mrs Smith for her welcome present of fruit, and the spirit in which she gave it.'

I SAY, I SAY

'I've just seen forty men under one umbrella and not one of them got wet.'
'It must have been a very large umbrella?'
'No. It wasn't raining.'

'It's all in the papers tonight.'
'What is?'
'Fish and chips.'

'If I post this letter tonight, will it get to Brighton in two days' time?'
'Well it might do – even in these days.'
'I bet you it won't.'
'Why not?'
'It's addressed to Southampton.'

'Those are pretty awful trousers you have on.'
'Yes, I call them my Arthur Scargill's.'
'Why?'
'Because they're not on very good terms with the press.'

'Where are you taking that basket of plums?'
'I'm taking them to Buckingham Palace for the Queen.'
'Why?'
'Because in "God Save The Queen" it says, "Send her Victorias." '

'I've just saved a girl from drowning.'
'How did it happen?'

'Well, I was walking along the beach when I saw a girl slowly drifting out to sea.'
'So you jumped in after her?'
'No I threw her a cake of soap.'
'Whatever for?'
'To wash her back of course.'

'I've just been up to Scotland on holiday. All the Scotsmen were wearing kilts.'
'Really. Did you see the Trussocks?'
'No. It wasn't windy.'

'My small nephew has got three feet.'
'Really. That's extraordinary. Has he always had them?'
'No. I got a letter from my sister this morning which said that I wouldn't recognise little Johnny now. He's grown another foot.'

'My mother hasn't been kissed by my father for ten years.'
'Why not?'
'She won't let him kiss her when he's drunk, and when he's sober he doesn't want to.'

'My brother swallowed his watch the other day and was rushed to the doctor.'
'What did the doctor do?'
'Told him to take some Epsom Salts to help pass the time away.'

'Isn't the weather terrible?'
'Yes. We've had a Madame Butterfly summer.'
'What do you mean?'
'One fine day.'

'My cows don't just produce milk, they make chocolate too.'
'That's ridiculous. Cows making chocolate. How on earth do they do that?'
'They drop it Rowntrees.'

(Very fast)

You're looking very smart. Where do you:

> 'Get your ties?'
> 'Thailand.'
> 'And your collars?'
> 'Colorado.'
> 'Your vests?'
> 'Vestminster.'
> 'Your pants?'
> 'Pannsylvania.'
> 'Your socks?'
> 'Sauchiehall Street.'
> 'Your shoes?'
> 'Sherusalem.'
> 'And your shirt. Where does that come from?'
> 'From the Isle of Man.'
> 'How do you know?'
> 'Because it hasn't got a tail.'

'I say. Do you know the difference between disappointment and despair?'
'No. I don't. What *is* the difference?'
'Well. Disappointment is the first time you discover you can't do it *twice*, and despair is the second time you find you can't do it *once*.'

'What's the difference between a woman in a short skirt getting out of a car and a rude joke?'
'I don't know. What *is* the difference?'
'Sometimes you see it, sometimes you don't.'

'I come of an old musical family. You know the great Handel?'
'Yes.'
'Well my father used to turn it.'

'Do you know the Epsom Salts song?'
'No. What is it?'
'Little man you've had a fizzy day.'

48

'What did you have for breakfast?'
'Haddock'
'Finnan?'
'No. Thick 'un.'

'Where were you born?'
'I was born on a ship at sea.'
'Really. I never knew that your mother had been on a ship.'
'She hadn't. I was travelling with a blonde friend of my father at the time.'

'He's so clever that we call him Fruit Salts.'
'Fruit Salts, why?'
'Enos.'

'I know a place where women only wear necklaces.'
'Where on earth is that?'
'Round the neck.'

'I went out with twin girls last night.'
'Did you have a good time?'
'Yes and no.'

A man went into a paper shop to buy some envelopes. There was an attractive girl behind the counter.
'Do you keep stationery, miss?' he asked.
'No, dear,' she replied. 'I wriggle a little bit.'

SPORTING LIFE

A little boy got lost at a football match. He went up to a policeman and said: 'I've lost my Dad.'

'What's he like?' asked the policeman sympathetically.

'Beer and women,' said the boy.

Arsenal were playing an Italian team in Italy before the war. Their half-back, Copping, did a tough sliding tackle on one of the Italian players. The Italian referee rushed up to Copping and said: 'None of that please. We want a sporting game.'

Five minutes later Copping did the same thing. This time the referee took his name and warned him that if he did it again he would be sent off. Another five minutes and Copping tripped yet another Italian player.

As he saw the referee approaching him, he muttered under his breath: 'Oh, bugger off.'

The referee heard him and said: 'Ah. That is good. You apologise. So I don't send you off.'

A centipede was playing for a team of insects, but came on to the field half an hour late. It took him longer than he thought it would to put on his boots.

A football team was having a disastrous season and their attendance figures had reached rock bottom. So much so that, before each match started, they used to introduce the crowd to the team. One day a man rang up and asked the manager what time the game started.

'What time can you get here?' was the manager's reply.

Jimmy Tarbuck tells the story of a friend of his who had a little white poodle. This poodle used to accompany his friend on all his games of golf. If his master did a good drive or sunk a long putt, the poodle would stand on his hind legs and applaud with his two front paws.

'What happens,' Jimmy asked his friend, 'if you get into a bunker or miss an easy putt?'

'Oh,' said his friend, 'the dog turns somersaults.'

'How many?' asked Jimmy.

'Depends how hard I kick him up the arse,' was the answer.

A very keen golfer used to play golf every day and the older he grew the more worried he became as to what it would be like up in heaven. Would there be any golf? So he thought he would consult a fortune-teller and asked her whether he would be able to play golf after he was dead.

She examined the cards carefully. Then checked with some tea-leaves. 'I've got the answer,' she said. 'There's good news and not such good news. The good news is that I can see a beautifully laid-out championship golf course with lush green fairways and perfect greens.'

'Good,' said the man, 'but, what's the bad news?'

'Well,' said the fortune-teller, 'I can see you teeing off the first tee *next* Thursday afternoon.'

A man had just played a game of golf at a strange golf course and rushed off to have a quick shower before going off to an important business appointment. He took his flannel into the shower and, after washing himself, was just about to step out to find a towel when, to his horror, he heard the sound of ladies' voices. He peeped out through the shower curtain and saw two elderly ladies and a smashing blonde. He realised that he had come into the ladies' shower room by mistake. But he had to get out of the shower as he had this important meeting to go to. So he thought that the only thing to do was to cover his face with the flannel and make a dash for it. He emerged stealthily from the shower and ran quickly past the three ladies, his face hidden by his flannel.

'I wonder who that was?' said one of the elderly ladies.

'Well, it wasn't my husband,' said the other.

'And it certainly wasn't mine,' said the first lady.

'And I can assure you,' said the blonde, 'that it wasn't any member of this club, either.'

A man got lost in a desert and hadn't had a drink of water for five days. He was in a terrible state; his tongue was hanging out, his clothes were in tatters and he could only muster sufficient strength to crawl through the sand. Suddenly he saw a caravan, so he crawled up to it and knocked on the door.

An Arab opened it and the man croaked out: 'Water, water. Please give me some water.'

'Sorry,' said the Arab. 'We have no water. Only ties. MCC tie, the Geoff Boycott testimonial tie, Cornhill tie – any tie you like.'

'No, no,' said the man as he crawled away. 'All I want is water.'

He struggled on a few more hundred yards and came on another caravan. Once again an Arab came to the door.

'Water, water,' croaked the man even more huskily. 'I must have water.'

'Sorry,' said the Arab. 'We have no water. Only ties. The Primary Club tie, Lords' Taverners' tie, the Free Forrester tie. Any tie you like.'

'No, no. I only want water,' blurted out the man with his tongue even more swollen in the heat.

He crawled away and had the same experience at two other caravans. It was ties, ties, ties – no water. In despair he crawled to the top of a sand-dune and, looking over the top, saw a verdant golf course laid out before him with lush fairways and greens. Surely, he thought, there must be water here. So, with one last effort he dragged himself up to the door of the white club house and knocked. A steward appeared and asked him what he wanted.

'I want water, water. Let me in, let me in,' he pleaded.

'I'm sorry, sir,' said the steward. 'You can't come in here without a tie.'

A golfer had just sunk a putt and stooped down to pick his ball out of the hole. As he did so a lady driving off a nearby tee sliced her drive badly and hit him hard on his bottom. He picked up her ball and took it to her.

'Madam,' he said. 'The hole at which you should be driving had a flag in it.'

A golfer used regularly to slice his drive into a bunker on the right of the green at the short sixteenth. When he died, they found that in his will he had asked that his ashes should be scattered in the middle of the sixteenth green – something he had never been able to achieve with his ball. So his widow took the casket up on to the course and stood on the edge of the sixteenth green. She took the lid off the casket and threw her husband's ashes towards the hole in the middle of the green. But it was a windy day and the ashes were blown straight into the bunker on the right of the green.

An unpopular secretary of a golf club was ill in hospital. He received a Get Well card from his committee to which a PS was added: 'The decision to send this card was approved by six votes to five.'

A golfer was ambidextrous. Some days he would play right-handed, some days left. One of his opponents asked him how he decided which way round he was going to play each time.
'Oh, it's easy,' he replied. 'If, when I wake up, my wife is lying on her right side, I play right-handed. If she's lying on her left side, then I play left-handed.'
'Ah,' said his friend. 'But what do you do if your wife wakes up lying on her back?'
'I ring up the golf club to say that I shall be an hour late,' was the swift reply.

A very keen golfer went on a cruise. The liner was sunk in a storm and the golfer was washed up on to a desert island. He was apparently the only survivor and was alone for about three days. Then a raft came into sight and on it was a glamorous blonde with a wonderful figure. She only had enough on to cover her confusion. She stepped ashore and was warmly greeted by the lone golfer and they were soon getting on handsomely together. The blonde cuddled up to him and stroked his bare chest.

'Would you like to play around with me?' she whispered in his ear.

'I would, very much,' replied the golfer. 'But, I'm afraid my golf clubs went down with the ship.'

An optimistic golfer always wore two pairs of socks whenever he played golf – just in case he ever got a hole in one.

A young man was due to play golf with his girlfriend. Before the game he went to the professional's shop and bought a couple of golf balls. He put them in his trouser pocket and met his girlfriend on the first tee. She noticed the bulge in his pocket and asked him what it was.

'It's only golf balls,' the young man replied.

'Oh,' she said. 'I'm sorry. Is it something like tennis elbow?'

BIRDS AND BEES

'Who's that girl I saw you with the other day?'
'It was a girl from the school.'
'Teacher?'
'No. It wasn't necessary.'

'She's a photographic sort of girl.'
'What's that?'
'Oh, she's underdeveloped, over-exposed and at her best in a dark room.'

Virginia went on a cruise recently. They called her Virgin for short – but not for long.

'Can I marry your daughter?'
'How much are you going to settle on her?'
'Oh, about 12 stone 6.'

'I've come to ask for your daughter's hand.'
'Well, you've had everything else. So you might as well have *that* as well.'

They nicknamed her spontaneous – she's always making up as she goes along.

She went on a cruise recently but thought it all bunk.

'That's a nice dress that girl's got on.'
'Yes. It's her religious dress.'
'What's that?'
'Lo(w) and behold.'

My girlfriend wears what I call a barbed wire dress. It protects the property without obscuring the view.

A girl got a job as a barmaid and became very friendly with some of her male customers. After six months she got the sack. She had pulled the wrong knob and got stout.

A girl got engaged to an Eskimo but she broke it off.

A man got engaged to a girl whilst sitting in his car in his garage, and then couldn't back out of it.

A young man went to ask his girlfriend's father whether he could marry her.
    'Certainly, dear boy. Of course you can. I'm delighted. But, I think I should warn you that she's got acute angina.'
    'You're telling me, sir,' replied the young man.

Learned young man to his girlfriend:
'Do you like Kipling?'
'I don't know,' she replied. 'I've never tried it.'

Same young man:
'What do you think of Dickens?'
'I don't know. I've never been to one.'

Two storks talking together:
'Any business today?'
'No. But, I put the wind up a couple of secretaries.'

The bride and bridegroom had been shown up to their honeymoon suite. It was 5 pm and they were feeling rather shy and awkward, and not too sure what to do. So the bridegroom asked the bride: 'Shall we go to bed now or shall we stay up late and watch the BBC TV 5.40 pm news?'

A young girl of 21 married an old man of 80. As they lay in bed on their first night she prayed: 'Oh, Lord, make me as old as my husband.'

And, even as she prayed, she felt old age creeping upon her.

A honeymoon couple had been lent a friend's house for their honeymoon. After the first night the bride went down to the kitchen to make breakfast. After a bit, she took the tray up to their bedroom. There were some delicious-looking bacon and eggs surrounded by a lot of lettuce.

'Thank you, darling. That looks lovely. But, why all the lettuce?'

'Oh,' said the bride, 'I want to see if you also *eat* like a rabbit.'

A young man was very nervous before the first night of his honeymoon, and wondered whether he would come up to scratch. His best man told him not to worry.

'Have a dozen oysters for supper and you'll be fine all night.'

The young man thanked him and went off on his honeymoon. When he got back he rang up his best man, who asked him how he had got on.

'Quite well, thank you. But not 100 per cent. I did as you suggested and had a dozen oysters, but only five of them worked.'

Another young bridegroom was equally nervous. He had never made love to a girl before and confided his worry to his best friend who was already married.

'Don't worry,' said the friend. 'Once in bed you'll soon find out what's what.'

So on the first night the bridegroom lay alongside his bride and started to stroke her body. After a bit he asked her: 'What's that?'

'What's what?' she said.

'Ah,' he sighed with relief. 'That's it.'

An elderly couple were celebrating their golden wedding and decided to spend a holiday at the hotel where they had spent their honeymoon.

'It will bring back such happy memories, dear,' said the wife. 'Do you remember how eager you were to make love to me? You just couldn't wait for me to undress. You didn't even give me time to get my stockings off.'

'Well, you needn't worry tonight,' replied her husband. 'You'll have time to knit yourself a pair.'

A man was asked if he had enjoyed his honeymoon.

'Yes, I certainly did,' he replied. 'I never knew you could have such fun without laughing.'

A businessman missed his last train and had to take the milk train which got him home about 4 am. All the lights were on in the house and when he opened the front door his wife was standing in the hall, obviously very distressed.

'Oh, thank God you've come home at last, darling,' she said. 'We have had a burglar in our bedroom.'

'Did he get anything?' asked the husband anxiously.

'Yes,' she said, 'that's the trouble. He did, I thought it was you!'

A young man gave his girlfriend a watch for her birthday. She was delighted and gave him a smacking kiss.

She then put the watch to her ear and, not hearing it tick, said, 'It's not going.'

'No,' said the young man, 'I'm giving you the works tonight.'

MOSES SUPPOSES

'Father, why can't I play sport like other boys? They all play football or cricket.'

'Be quiet, Ikey. I know what's good for you. Now deal those cards.'

Two Jewish passengers on a cruise received a note in their sumptuous cabin asking them to sit at the captain's table.

'My God,' said the husband to his wife. 'I've paid big money for this cruise and now they ask us to eat with the crew.'

'Mr Cohen,' said the bank manager on the phone. 'Your overdraft now stands at £200. It's been like that since June. What are you going to do about it?'

'What was it at the end of May?'

'You were in credit with us to the tune of £500.'

'So. Did I ring you?'

A Jewish couple won £250,000 on the pools. They were obviously delighted but the wife had one worry.

'What about all the begging letters?' she asked her husband.

'Continue sending them, my dear,' was his reply.

A young recruit for the Jewish army was asked by the officer who interviewed him: 'Would you like a commission?'

'No thanks. I'd sooner have a straight salary.'

A lady was weeping by the side of a tombstone in a cemetery. The rabbi came up to try to comfort her.

'It's my husband,' she explained. 'I miss him terribly.'

'Your husband?' queried the rabbi. 'But it says on the gravestone: "To the memory of Rachel Cohen." '

'Yes,' sobbed the lady. 'He always put everything in my name.'

A landlord knocked on the door of a Jewish tenant.

'Good morning, Ikey,' he said. 'I've come to tell you that I'm going to raise the rent.'

'Thank the good Lord,' said Ikey, 'because I can't.'

Isaac told his solicitor: 'Insert a clause in my will which says that when I die I want all my relations to come and dance on my grave. And, by the way, make sure you remember to bury me at sea.'

Abie's wife noticed that he was obviously very worried about something. He couldn't sleep, had lost his appetite and wore a permanent worried look. After a few days she asked him what was wrong.

'It's awful my dear,' said Abie. 'I owe Benjamin £500. I can't pay it back and I daren't tell him. I don't know what to do.'

'Why don't you ring him up straightaway and tell him so. Then *he*'ll do the worrying, not you.'

A Jewish boy and a Catholic boy were having a quarrel.

'Our priest knows more than your rabbi,' said the Catholic.

'He should do,' said the Jew. 'You're always telling him everything.'

LUCK OF THE IRISH

The Irish winner of the famous Tour de France went missing for three weeks. He was found doing a lap of honour.

There was the Irish tug-of-war team which was disqualified for pushing.

The Irishman asked the attendant at the car wash how much it would cost.
'20p for you Paddy.'
'How did you know that I was an Irishman?'
'Well, we don't get too many through here on motorbikes.'

There were two Irishmen stranded on an iceberg.
'Look Paddy,' said one, 'we're saved. Here comes the *Titanic*.'

An Irishman applied to join the fire brigade. When asked why he wanted to join, he said that his wife had told him to go to blazes.

Two Irish gravediggers went on strike. They decided only to deal with emergency cases.

An Irishman bought a black and white dog as he thought the licence would be cheaper.

The Irish Water Polo Team would have done better had three of their horses not drowned.

61

An Irish stunt driver tried to drive a bus over twenty-five motorcycles. He would have succeeded but halfway over someone rang the bell.

The Irish hitchhiker got up early and made an early start on his journey. He wanted to miss the traffic.

The Irish harpoonist won the Miss W(h)ales competition.

An Irishman drove his car into a river because the local policeman told him to dip his headlights.

An Irishman was found drinking a glass of beer on the roof of a pub. When asked why he said he'd been told that drinks were on the house.

An Irishman was told by the IRA to blow up a certain car. But he burnt his lips on the exhaust.

An Irish motorist got his car stuck in a church door. He'd been told to take his car in for a service.

An Irishman thought that a Royal Enfield was a place where the Queen kept her chickens.

An Irish bobsleigh team was competing in the Winter Olympic Games. But there was a terrible crash. The Austrian team met the Irish team coming *up*.

An Irish cricketer caught a brilliant catch at third slip – but missed it on the action replay.

An Irishman applied for a job in a factory which made false noses. So they gave him a job as a picket.

An Irishman was accused of raping a girl and was lined up in an identity parade. The girl was brought into the prison yard where the row of men were standing and the Irishman pointed at her and said: 'That's her.'

An Irishman came home unexpectedly and found his wife in the arms of his best friend. He rushed to a drawer, took out a revolver and pointed it at his head.

'This is too much,' he cried. 'I'm going to shoot myself.'

At this, his wife began to laugh.

'I don't know what you are laughing at,' he said to her, 'you're next.'

An Irishman driving a horse-box arrived at a race-course. A stable lad opened the door.

'There's no horse in here, Paddy,' he called out.

'No,' said Paddy. 'I bring the non-runners.'

An Englishman, a Scotsman and an Irishman were lost in a sandstorm in the desert. Suddenly a genie appeared and told them that they could each have one wish.

The Englishman said he would like to be back home in his cottage in the Cotswolds, and was immediately transported there in a flash.

The Scotsman asked if he could go to his small croft in the Highlands, and immediately he was whisked away there.

The genie turned to the Irishman and asked him what his wish was.

'I'm feeling lonely without my two friends. Could I have them back here please?'

A notice outside an Irish undertaker's office read: 'Due to the holidays, for the next week we shall be working with a skeleton staff.'

Then there was the Irishman who thought a polythene bag was a Greek tart.

An Irishman was lying on the ground peering down a rabbit-hole. A passer-by asked him what on earth he was doing.

'Oh, I'm the borough surveyor,' the Irishman replied.

At a level-crossing in Ireland only one of the gates was open. A motorist asked the level-crossing keeper the reason.

'Oh, you see sir, we are half expecting a train.'

An Irishman rang up London Airport and asked how long the air flight to Dublin took.

'Just a minute, sir,' said the operator.

'Thank you,' said the Irishman and rang off.

A Letter from an Irish Mother to her Son

Dear Son,

I've forgot your address, so if you don't receive this, let me know. If you don't let me know I'll know that you've got it.

Just a few lines to let you know I'm still alive. I'm writing this letter slowly because I know you can't read fast. You won't know the house when you get home; we've moved.

About your father. He has a lovely new job, he has 500 men under him, he cuts grass at the cemetery. There was a washing-machine at the new house when we moved in but it hasn't been working too good. Last week I put 14 shirts in, pulled the chain and haven't seen the shirts since.

Your sister Mary had a baby this morning but I haven't found out whether it's a boy or a girl, so I don't know if you are an aunt or an uncle.

Your Uncle Patrick drowned last week in a vat of whiskey in the Dublin Brewery. Some of his workmates tried to save him but he

64

fought them off bravely. They cremated him and it took three days to put out the fire.

I went to the doctor on Thursday and your father went with me. The doctor put a small tube in my mouth and told me not to talk for ten minutes. Your father offered to buy it from him.

It only rained twice this week, first for three days and then for four days. Monday was so windy one of the chickens laid the same egg four times. We had a letter from the undertaker. He said if the last payment on your grandmother's plot wasn't paid in seven days, up she comes.

Your loving mother

PS I was going to send you a quid for your birthday, but I had already sealed the envelope.
PPS I'll see you in the same place on Sunday. If I'm there first I'll put a chalk mark on the wall, if you're there first, rub it out.

An Irishman was stopped by a foreign tourist and asked what the yellow line along the side of the street indicated.

'Oh, that means no parking at all.'

'Thank you,' said the tourist. 'But, what do *two* yellow lines mean?'

'Ah,' said the Irishman, 'That means no parking at all, at all.'

Paddy was woken up by the phone ringing. So he got out of bed, went downstairs, and picking up the phone said:

'Hello?'

'Hello. Is that Belfast double two, double two?'

'No. I'm sorry. This is Belfast two, two, two, two.'

'Oh. I'm sorry to have troubled you.'

'It's all right,' said Paddy. 'I had to come down anyway as the phone was ringing.'

A customer in an Irish restaurant asked for some coffee at the end of his meal.

'With cream or without?' asked the Irish waiter.

'Without cream, thank you,' said the customer.

65

After a short delay the waiter returned. 'I'm sorry, sir. There is no more cream. Will you have it without milk?'

Then there was the Irish sheep-dog trial. They were all found guilty.

The pilot of a large jet travelling from New York to London announced over the intercom: 'I'm sorry. We are having engine trouble and I've had to shut down number one engine. Nothing to worry about. It will just mean we shall be fifteen minutes late arriving at Heathrow.'

A few minutes later the pilot came on the intercom again: 'Ladies and gentlemen. I'm sorry. I've just had to shut down number two engine, which is giving a bit of trouble. But don't worry. It will just mean that we shall now be thirty minutes late.'

A few minutes later he came on again. 'It's your captain speaking again. I'm sorry but I've now had to shut down number three engine which means we may be up to an hour late.'

An Irish passenger turned to the man sitting next to him and said: 'I hope he doesn't have to shut down the fourth engine, or we shall be up here all night.'

An Irishman visited his doctor who gave him a bottle of tonic. Two weeks later the Irishman went back to the doctor saying he felt no better.

'Have you been taking the medicine I gave you, Paddy?' asked the doctor.

'No,' said Paddy.

'Why not?' asked the doctor.

'Well, when I got home I looked at the bottle and there was a label on it which said: "Keep this bottle tightly corked." So I did.'

An Irishman was wearing a pair of shoes of which one was brown, the other black.

A friend noticed them and said: 'A pair of different coloured shoes, Paddy. That must be unique?'

'Oh no,' said Paddy. 'I've got another pair just like them at home.'

An Irish foreman told an Irish worker to measure the height of a flagpole. He returned after half an hour and saw that the worker had cut down the flagpole and was measuring it as it lay on the ground.

'What on earth are you doing? Why have you cut the pole down? I didn't ask you to measure its width.'

Jokes

Have you heard of the Irishman who:

wanted to buy a house – he went to British Home Stores.

thought that Ellesmere Port was a new type of dinner wine.

stole a calendar – he got twelve months.

was ironing the curtains – he kept falling out of the window.

drove his lorry off Beachy Head to test the air brakes.

drove in the Indianapolis 500 and had thirty-two pit stops – one for petrol and thirty-one to ask the way.

went to the dentist to have a wisdom tooth put in.

got a pair of water skis for Christmas – he spent a year looking for a lake on a slope.

bought a paper shop – it blew away.

crashed his helicopter – he switched off the fans because he could not stand the draught.

found a milk churn in the hedgerow – he thought it was a cow's nest.

got a job sweeping up leaves in Hyde Park – he fell out of the tree and broke his leg.

was studying Greek mythology – when asked what was half man and half beast, replied: 'Could it be Buffalo Bill?'

bought a pair of wellies – he took them back two days later for a longer piece of string.

entered for two events in the 1980 Olympics – heading the shot and catching the javelin.

was a kamikaze pilot – writing his memoirs.

was asked on 'University Challenge', 'Where are the Andes?' and replied, 'On the end of my wristies.'

was asked, 'What was Ghandi's first name,' and replied, 'Could it be Goosey Goosey.'

was asked, 'What are hippies?' and replied, 'Could they be to hang your leggies on?'

thought that Sherlock Holmes was a block of flats.

thought that Sheffield Wednesday was a Bank Holiday.

An Irishman's wife wanted a coat made of animal skin – he bought her a donkey jacket.

An Irishman killed himself jumping off an office block after the foreman told him that he flew Wellingtons during the war.

Have you heard about:

the Irish firing squad – it formed a circle.

the Irish tap dancer – he fell in the sink.

the Irishman whose wife gave birth to triplets – he is looking for the other two fathers.

the Irish Humpty Dumpty – the wall fell on *him*.

the Irish fish – it drowned.

the Irish parachute – it opens on impact.

How do you define 144 Irishmen? Gross stupidity.

Why are there only twenty hours in the Irish day? Have you ever seen an Irishman with twenty-four fingers and toes!

How do you tell an Irish Father Christmas? Sack full of Easter eggs.

Why are camels in Egypt and Paddys in Ireland? The Arabs had first choice.

Why should there be oil in Egypt and potatoes in Ireland? The Irish had first choice.

You can always tell an Irishman in Holland – he's the one with the wooden wellies.

Four Irishmen were sitting in a circle smoking. Police stated later that they had smashed a dope ring.

An Aer Lingus pilot, when asked for his height and position replied: 'I'm 5 ft 4 in and sitting in the front seat.'

An Irishman fell 3,000 ft down a well. Murphy shouted, 'Are you all right?' The Irishman replied, 'I haven't broken anything, there is nothing to break down here.'

How do you brainwash an Irishman? Fill his wellies full of water.

What do you get if you cross an Irishman with a pig? Thick bacon.

How do you pick out the Irishmen on the oil rigs? They are the ones trying to feed bread to the helicopter.

How do you confuse an Irishman? Give him twelve shovels and tell him to take his pick.

How do you tell a level-headed Irishman? He dribbles from both sides of his mouth at the same time.

How do you get an Irishman to burn his ears? Phone him when he's ironing.

What do you call a pregnant Irish woman? A dope carrier.

What do you call an Irishman on a bike? A dope peddler.

How do you tell an Irish solicitor? Pin-striped donkey jacket and wellies.

Have you heard of the Irish window-cleaner cleaning the outside of windows on a skyscraper? He stepped back to admire his work.

An Irishman visited a chiropodist and asked him to examine a painful corn. 'Me fate is in your hands,' he said.

I PUT IT TO YOU

A girl in a rape case was finding the cross-examination of the barrister very embarrassing and was making no sense with her replies. It was nearing the interval for lunch, so the judge thought he would try to help her.

'Just tell us, in your own words, my dear, exactly what happened.'

'Well, m'lord,' the girl stammered out slowly. 'My boyfriend took me into a field and we lay down. He then lifted up my skirt and put his hand inside my knickers . . . .'

'And there,' said the judge, looking at his watch, 'I think we will leave it until two o'clock.'

A judge was about to sentence a prisoner who had been found guilty.

'Is there anything you want to say before I sentence you, my man?' he asked.

'Bugger all, m'lord,' replied the prisoner.

The judge, who was a bit hard of hearing, called down to his clerk of the court: 'What did he say?'

'Bugger all, m'lord,' answered the clerk.

'No,' said the judge. 'He definitely said something. I saw him move his lips.'

Three magistrates were trying a rape case. It was a hot afternoon and the courtroom was stuffy. The chairman was a lady. On her right was an alert businessman and on her left was a retired colonel with a bristling white military moustache. He began to nod off and was soon fast asleep as the chairman asked the young girl in the witness box to write down what the accused man had said to her. The girl wrote something down on a piece of paper which was handed up to the chairman, who read it and then handed it to the man on her right. He then passed it back to her and she gently nudged the sleeping colonel to wake him up. He gave a slight snort and woke up to find the following note being passed to him by the lady chairman.

'I'm feeling randy. What about coming back to my place for a quick one?'

He read it with horror and handed it back to the chairman, whispering: 'Madam. Control yourself. You must be out of your mind.'

What was the nickname given to a well-known judge who had lost a thumb? Mr Justice Fingers.

'Remember you are on oath,' said the judge to the third party in a divorce case. 'Answer me this. Have you ever slept with this woman?'

'Not a wink, m'lord,' was the reply.

Judge: 'Is this the first time you've been up before me?'
Prisoner: 'I don't know, m'lord. What time do you usually get up?'

A farmer was talking to his solicitor before a case. The solicitor assured the farmer that he would get him off.

'But would it help if I sent the judge a couple of ducks?' asked the farmer.

'Good gracious, no. That would go against you. The judge would consider it bribery.'

After the case the solicitor congratulated the farmer when he was found not guilty. 'There you are,' he said. 'I told you I would get you off.'

'Yes, I know,' said the farmer. 'But, I sent the two ducks in the other chap's name.'

72

A man was up before a magistrate for misbehaving with his dog.

'This is a dreadful case,' said the magistrate. 'I really don't know what to do with you.'

Voice from the back of the court: 'Give him the cat.'

SOLDIER, SAILOR

Officer on an exercise at Royal Military Academy, Sandhurst: 'Brown. If you were in charge of a platoon defending this ridge, and suddenly saw ten enemy tanks approaching you up the hill, what steps would you take?'
Brown: 'Bloody long ones, sir.'

A commanding officer was addressing his troops before embarking for an overseas posting. He was stressing the dangers of VD abroad. 'Why spoil your health for just ten minutes' pleasure? Any questions?' A young soldier held up his hand.
CO: 'Yes? What do you want to know?'
Young soldier: 'Please sir? How do you make it last *that long*?'

A very ugly officer had done wonderful work when attached to the Free French Army. He would have been given the Croix de Guerre, but the French could not find a general prepared to kiss him.

A young subaltern joined his new regiment and was warmly welcomed by his commanding officer.
CO: 'Welcome to the regiment and, so that you can get to know everybody, I've arranged a party in the mess tonight. A little drink never did anyone any harm.'
Subaltern: 'I'm sorry, sir, but I don't drink.'
CO: 'Don't worry about that then, on Wednesday night we'll get a few girls up to the mess from the NAAFI. A bit of slap and tickle does one a power of good.'
Subaltern: 'Sorry, sir. I don't approve of that sort of thing.'

74

CO: (looking at the subaltern quizzically) 'Er . . . you aren't by any chance a queer, are you?'
Subaltern: 'Certainly not, sir.'
CO: 'Pity. You won't enjoy Saturday night either.'

At a regimental dinner a few years after the war, one officer said to another: 'Nice to see you old boy. How are you?'

'Oh, I'm alright, but feeling rather frustrated with my sex life. I haven't made love to a woman since 1945.'

'Well,' said the first officer, looking at his watch. 'I don't know what you are worried about. It's only 20.15 now.'

Won't Live Long

Customer: *'Waiter, there's a fly in my soup!'*
Waiter:

'It's all right, sir, he won't live long in that stuff.'

'That's funny – most people find cockroaches.'

'Leave it there, sir, and I'll fetch the goldfish.'

'Really? So that's where they go in winter, is it?'

'One moment, sir, and I'll call the spider.'

'Please don't wave your spoon about like that – you'll frighten the poor thing.'

'Don't scream, sir, everybody will want one.'

Waiter: 'Would you like aperitif, sir?'
Diner: 'No thanks. I always use my own dentures.'

Diner: 'Waiter, have you got frogs' legs?'
Waiter: 'Yes, sir.'
Diner: 'Well, hop over there and get me the mustard, please.'

Waiter: 'Would you like a salad, sir?'
Diner: 'Yes please. I'll have a honeymoon salad.'
Waiter: 'Honeymoon salad, sir. What is that?'
Diner: 'Lettuce alone without dressing.'

'Waiter, do you serve crabs in this restaurant?'
'Yes, sir, sit down. We serve anyone here.'

A waiter was scratching his bottom.
'Excuse me asking,' exclaimed a concerned lady diner, 'but have you got haemorrhoids?'
'No, madam. I'm sorry,' replied the waiter. 'Only what's on the menu.'

'Waiter, what on earth is this soup?'
'It's bean soup, sir.'
'I don't care what it's *been*, what is it now?'

A waiter brought a customer the lobster which he had ordered. But it only had one claw. The customer noticed this and asked where the other claw was. The waiter had to think quickly.
'When they arrived this morning they were still alive, and two of them started fighting, and this one lost a claw in the fight.'
'OK,' said the customer. 'Then bring me the winner.'

The waiter presented the menu to a young man and his girlfriend.
'What do you suggest?' asked the young man. 'I've only got £10.'
'Another restaurant, sir,' said the waiter.

'Waiter. How long will my sausages be?'
'I don't know, sir. We never measure them.'

Waiter: 'How would you like your coffee, sir?'
Diner: (facetiously) 'The same way as I like my women. Hot, strong and very sweet.'
Waiter: 'Black or white, sir?'

FAMILY FEELINGS

'My wife has just died. I shall miss her. She was one in a million.'
'Really. I thought she was won in a raffle.'

'Here's a letter from my wife.'
'But there's nothing written on it.'
'No. We're not on speaking terms.'

'I've just divorced my wife.'
'Why?'
'She's got flat feet.'
'But you can't divorce a woman for having flat feet.'
'Yes you can. She kept on putting them in the wrong flat.'

'My wife's a regular first-nighter.'
'Keen on the theatre?'
'No. She's been married six times.'

'I've just got six months for rocking my wife to sleep.'
'But you can't get six months for that.'
'Well . . . you should have seen the size of the rock.'

'I call my wife Radio 4.'
'Why?'
'Because she never has anything on after midnight.'

'My wife doesn't like soft sugar.'
'What do you do about it?'
'Make her lump it!'

'Where are you going?'
'I'm going to fetch the doctor. I don't like the look of my wife.'
'I'll come with you. I hate the sight of mine.'

'My wife's just left me.'
'Oh, really. How much?'

'Where's your wife these days?'
'She's gone to the West Indies.'
'Jamaica?'
'No. She went of her own accord.'

'My wife has gone to Indonesia.'
'Jakarta?'
'No. She went by plane.'

'I'm off to China.'
'Hangkhow?'
'No. I'm leaving her behind.'

'How's your pain in the neck?'
'Oh, she's staying with her mother.'

'Where's your wife?'
'She's in bed with sciatica.'
'Not that damned Italian again!'

'My wife's in hospital.'
'Flu?'
'Yes – and crashed.'

79

'My brother has just divorced his wife.'
'On what grounds?'
'The recreation grounds.'

'Did you know that Jim has died?'
'No I didn't. What were his last words?'
'There weren't any. His wife was there.'

'My wife drives me to drink.'
'You're lucky. I have to walk to my pub.'

'What will you have to drink?'
'A mother-in-law please.'
'What on earth is that?'
'Stout and bitter.'

'What's your uncle doing these days?'
'Oh, he's in low water.'
'Oh, I'm sorry.'
'No, not to worry. He gives swimming lessons. He's a contortionist –
he can swim with one foot on the bottom.'

'I call my brother Button B.'
'Why?'
'He's always pressed for money.'

'My son is an electrician and I don't like it.'
'Why?'
'Well, he's always wiring for money.'

'What's the weather like today?'
'Oh, it's grandmother weather – wet and windy.'

'My love for my wife is like a kangaroo with rheumatism – it knows
no bounds.'

'We call my father label.'
'Why?'
'He sticks so close to the bottle.'

'We've nicknamed our uncle Jerry.'
'Why?'
'Because all the women sit on him, and the men hold him at arms' length.'

My brother's got a Rolls-Royce nose. It runs silently.

My uncle George has barometeritis – the glass keeps going up and down.
He's got alcoholic constipation – he can't pass a pint.

My father's got commercial traveller eyes – look at the bags under them.

'I'm just off to see my brother. He's taking part in a six-day bicycle race.'
'But, that finished two days ago.'
'I know – I'm going to tell him.'

I've got a Canadian cousin who's so cross-eyed that he spent two years in the south-east trying to join the north-west mounted police.

My brother eats so much fish that his stomach keeps going in and out with the tide.

His nerves are so bad that every time he sees a bit of cotton it makes him reel.

'What's your brother doing these days?'
'Nothing.'

81

'Oh, I thought he had applied for that job at Methuen.'

'Yes. He got the job.'

'He's lucky. *My* brother's unemployed. Even so he lives above his income.'

'Surely he can't do that?'

'Oh yes. He's got a flat over the Social Security office.'

A husband and wife were arguing about money – or the lack of it.

'We've simply got to economise somehow,' said the husband. 'If only you could cook, we could sack the cook.'

'In that case,' said the wife, 'if you could make love properly, we could also sack the chauffeur.'

A man met his wife-to-be in a travel agent's. He was looking through the brochures and she was the last resort.

A young boy and his father went to spend a penny in a public lavatory.

The young boy came out first and his mother, who was waiting for them, asked: 'Where's your Dad?'

'Oh, it's all right Mum,' the boy replied. 'Dad said he would be out in a couple of shakes.'

'My mother and father are in the iron and steel business.'

'Really? I didn't know that.'

'Yes. My mother irons and my father steals.'

A man always told people that his cockney wife was really a Scandinavian. When they expressed their surprise he explained that: 'She eats like a Norse.'

'For twenty years my wife and I were very happy.'

'What happened then?'

'We met.'

'Who was that lady I saw you with last night?'
'That was no lady. It was my brother. He walks that way.'

A married couple had ten children in the first twelve years of their
marriage. The trouble was that the wife was stone deaf and whenever
her husband said: 'Shall we go to sleep or what?' she always said:
'What?'

A woman married a man who was deaf and dumb. At night she
insisted on him wearing boxing gloves to stop him talking in bed.

A man had a rather frigid wife. So one day he took her out and gave
her a slap-up dinner with plenty to drink. When they got home he
gave her two aspirins.
  'But, darling, I feel fine. I haven't got a headache,' she said.
  'Right,' he said, 'let's go straight up to bed and make love.'

A rather short-sighted social worker knocked on the door of a house.
A small boy came to the door. The conversation went as follows:
  'Is your father in?'
  'No, he went out when my mother came in.'
  'Is your mother in, then?'
  'No, she went out when my brother came in.'
  'Can I see him then please?'
  'No. I'm afraid not. He went out when I came in.'
  'So, you are left in charge of the house?'
  'Oh, no. This is not our house. It's our outside lavatory.'

An old man summoned his young wife and told her: 'I must have an
heir. I must have heir.'
  His young wife took his hand and said gently: 'Darling, you may
be heir-minded, but I'm afraid you are not heir-conditioned.'

A man dreaded his mother-in-law coming to stay. She was such a
know-all. Whatever he said, she would say: 'I know, I know.'

83

He might have heard the late news on the TV, or read a headline in the paper. No matter what it was, if he mentioned it, back came the reply, 'I know, I know.'

When he learnt from his wife that her mother was coming to stay for Christmas, he had an idea. One morning he went out to the milkman who had just driven up in his milk cart.

'Will you hire me your horse for Christmas morning? I will pay you anything reasonable. I shall only need him for about an hour before breakfast on Christmas Day.'

The milkman agreed terms and early on Christmas morning made the man's house his last call. He and the man unharnessed the horse and the man asked the milkman if he would help him take the horse inside the house, then take him upstairs and finally put him in the bath. After a great struggle they achieved this, damaging a lot of the paintwork up the stairs. But they managed it without waking anyone in the house. When they got downstairs, the man gave the milkman a cup of tea; the latter was naturally a bit perplexed.

'Why on earth do you want to put a horse in the bath?' asked the man.

'Well, it's like this,' said the man. 'My mother-in-law is staying with us. Whatever I say she always answers with: 'I know, I know.' So, when she gets up this morning she will go to the bathroom and she will scream and come rushing out, shouting: 'Help, help. There's a horse in the bath,' and I shall say, casually: 'I know, I know.'

A husband and wife were quarrelling.

'I was just thinking what to put on your tombstone,' he said.

'What about: "Wife of the above"?' said his wife.

A young man and his fiancée were taking a walk in the woods. They sat down under a tree and after a short while the inevitable happened. Afterwards the girl cried bitterly.

'Oh, I feel such a sinner doing it before we are married. I don't know how I can face my parents after being so wicked twice in an afternoon.'

'Twice?' said the young man. 'We only did it once.'

'Oh, but you *are* going to do it again aren't you?' she said.

A husband and wife were discussing what would happen when one of them died.

'Will you remarry, darling?' asked the wife.

'No. I don't think so,' said the husband.

'But I would like you to, and if you do, give her all my jewellery.'

'Don't talk like that, darling,' he said.

'No, I mean it,' said the wife, 'even though you've got no-one in mind now, you will soon find someone to take my place. And, when you do, you can also give her my golf clubs.'

'No. That wouldn't work, darling. She's left-handed.'

A mother of eight young children was sitting stitching up her husband's pyjamas when a friend came in and asked her why she was doing it.

'A stitch in time saves nine,' was the reply.

Some visitors were going round the Chamber of Horrors at Madame Tussaud's. An attendant approached one of them and pointed to a woman who was standing still staring at one of the gruesome exhibits.

'Excuse me, sir, is that lady anything to do with you?'

'Yes,' said the man. 'She's my mother-in-law.'

'Well, please keep her moving. We're stock-taking,' said the attendant.

A man boasted to a friend: 'Last night for the first time in ten years my wife and I reached sexual compatability. We *both* had headaches!'

A wife was a bit worried about her sex life with her husband, so bought him a book on sex for Christmas. In the New Year she asked him if he had picked up any tips which would help make their sex together more satisfactory.

'Yes,' he said. 'There was an article which said how much it helped if the woman moaned during the climax of the act. Let's try it tonight.'

So, when things were going well later that night, his wife whispered: 'Is this the moment? Shall I start to moan now?'

'Yes,' he replied in a husky voice. 'Start now.'

'Right,' said the wife. 'Why on earth do you always leave me to do all the washing up?'

A man who worked in an office was always interfering in other people's business. He would make suggestions, offer advice and generally try to organise everything that went on. He even went so far as to try out his ideas on the managing director, who somewhat naturally resented it, and gave the man an almighty rocket. But the man misunderstood what he meant and rushed home to his wife.

'Darling, I've some great news. I've been promoted. The managing director has made me his sexual adviser.'

'Oh, wonderful darling. I'm *so* pleased. What did he say to you to break the news?'

'Well, he rose to his feet and accompanied me to the door, talking so fast that I couldn't hear much of what he was saying. But I did hear the important part. As I went out of the door he said: "When I want your f——g advice, I'll ask for it." '

The young son of a clergyman was always swearing. So his father told him what a great sin it was in the eyes of God.

'Promise me that every time you swear you will give five shillings to the person nearest to you?'

The boy promised but the next morning on his way to school he tripped over a bucket which the pretty young maid was using to scrub the floor.

'Who put that bloody bucket there?' he shouted. He then remembered his promise and, seeing the blushing young maid, gave her five shillings.

'Cor blimey,' she said. 'Like father, like son. Where do you want it? In the front room or up in the attic?'

A wife was telling her husband about her trip to the cinema.

'I had to move my seat five times.'

'Why? Were you molested?'

'Yes,' she replied. 'Eventually.'

A man returned home one night and found that his wife had two black eyes.

'Who gave you those?' he asked.

'The lodger gave them to me.'

So the husband went up to the lodger's room and asked him: 'Is that right? You gave my wife two black eyes?'

'Yes, I certainly did,' said the lodger. 'She's been unfaithful to us.'

A boy told his father that he wanted to get married.

'Very well, son. Whom do you want to marry?'

'Miss Green, dad.'

'You can't marry her. She's your half-sister. When I was a lad, I had a bike and used to get around a bit.'

'All right, then, dad. I'll marry Miss White.'

'You can't do that either. She's also your half-sister.'

The boy was very despondent and told his mum that his dad said that he couldn't marry Miss Green or Miss White as they were his half-sisters.

'You go and marry which of them you like,' said his mum. 'He's not your father anyway.'

'Greengables'
17 Marsh Lane
Mill Hill
London

10.12.80

Dear Mummy and Daddy,

I want to thank you both for bringing me up the way you have, for encouraging me to make my own decisions and to speak my mind. This somehow makes it easier for me to write this letter.

As you know, I am 16 now and old enough to know my own mind and hope you will not be too upset when I tell you that I am deeply in love with a 42-year-old Jamaican called Ewan.

He has been married before, twice, but his second divorce should be coming through soon. Ewan feels that he will probably be asked to pay something in the region of £40 a week towards the upkeep of his eight children, and as he is out of work at the moment, this means that I will probably have to go out to work. However, Ewan tells me that he knows of a job where I could make much more than this every week and he tells me that I would probably even learn to enjoy it in time. However, he has promised to tell me more of that later.

We went to see his doctor last night and he has assured us that once Ewan has got over one or two little things that he has picked up recently we can really start living together properly.

Ewan has for a long time been dissatisfied with the climate of opinion in this country towards one of his background and some time ago applied for emigration to Canada. He has just been notified that he has been accepted and the papers are in the post, so by the time you get back we shall probably be on the high seas *en route* for Newfoundland.

Dearest mummy and daddy, none of this that I have told you is true, but I have just found out that I failed my 'O' levels and I wanted you to get everything in perspective.

Yours,

Debbie.

'Have you got a good job?'
'Yes. I get a very good salary, but I give it all to my wife.'
'But, there's no law against keeping some for yourself.'
'Oh yes there is. Mother-in-law.'

A man was going out to dinner wearing his dinner jacket. His young daughter called after him:

'Daddy why have you got that black and white suit on again? You know it always gives you a headache in the morning.'

A woman was asking a friend how her marriage was going and whether she was happy with her husband.

'I don't know what to say dear,' said her friend. 'Bert works very hard at his garage and I think he's doing too much. The job is getting on top of him. The other night in bed I woke up and found he was stroking my bottom and saying: "Disgraceful. Only 5,000 miles and the tread has gone already."

88

A lady was applying for a divorce.

'What is your relationship with your husband?'

'Terrible, m'lord.'

'Is he a friendly man?'

'M'lord, I've been married to him for four years and he's only spoken to me three times.'

'Hmm,' said the judge looking at his papers. 'It looks a clear case. Divorce granted. And I give you custody of the three children.'

A man came home unexpectedly and found a completely naked man talking to his wife on the sofa. He was furious.

'What's he doing here?'

'It's all right, darling. It's a nudist who has come in to use the phone.'

A man went to see his doctor about his sex life. His wife was complaining that he was too demanding and wanted sex far too often.

'What shall I do, doctor? I can't help my sexual appetite.'

'I'd recommend that you should always have a glass of water by your bed and drink it every night.'

'Before or after, doctor?'

'Instead.'

When his wife died a Yorkshireman asked the stonemason to carve on her tombstone the words: 'She was Thine.'

Some weeks after the funeral he went up to the churchyard and, to his annoyance, saw the following words on his wife's tombstone: 'She was Thin.'

He rang up the stonemason and complained that the 'e' had been left out. The mason apologised and said that he would rectify the mistake as soon as possible.

A week later the husband returned to his wife's grave and read the alteration that had been made: 'E, she was thin.'

A little boy was kneeling by his bedside. His father came up to say goodnight, and seeing his son apparently saying his prayers, knelt down on the other side of the bed.

'What are you doing, dad?' asked the small boy.

'Just the same as you my son,' replied his father sanctimoniously.

'I shouldn't if I were you,' said the boy. 'You won't half cop it from mum. There's only one chamber-pot under the bed and I'm using it at the moment.'

Two young wives were discussing the sexual prowess of their respective husbands. One of them complained that her's was not too good.

'Oh,' said the other, 'mine was the same a year ago. But I made him take some rhino-horn pills and ever since then his performance has been magnificent.'

Her friend thanked her and said she would get her husband to take the pills also. They met a month or two later and the friend who had suggested the pills asked how they had worked.

'Oh, absolutely marvellously. He has become an insatiable lover. But I do have one worry. When we are out walking, every time he sees a Land Rover he tries to charge it.'

WHY DID THE CHICKEN...?

Why are policemen so strong?
They can hold up the traffic with one hand.

What would happen to the economy if pigs could fly?
Bacon would go up.

If you were standing stark naked in a snowstorm, what animal would you like to be?
A little otter.

Who were the ice-cream men in the Bible?
Walls of Jericho and Lyons of Judah.

If a Frenchman is shot out of a cannon, what's his name?
Napoleon Blownapart.

What's the shape of a kiss?
Eliptical.

Do you know the difference between (Raquel Welch) and the Hudson River?
No. I haven't been up the Hudson River.

What's the difference between funny and fanny?
Well, you can feel funny without feeling fanny, but you can't feel fanny without feeling funny.

What's the difference between a gentleman and a knight?
Once a gentleman, always a gentleman. Once a (k)night – dead at forty.

If a cat has kittens on a pillow, are they caterpillars?

What's got six eyes and can't see?
Three blind mice.

What do you call a deaf elephant?
Anything you like. He won't hear you.

If your house is overrun by homosexual mice, what do you do?
Get a puffy cat.

What lies shivering at the bottom of the sea?
A nervous wreck.

How do porcupines make love?
Very carefully.

How do you get down off an elephant?
You don't. You get it from a swan.

Who was the most elastic man in the Bible?
Balaam – because he tied his ass to a tree and then walked to Jerusalem.

If a fly flying to China passed a flea flying to London, what would be the time in China when they passed each other?
Fly past flea.

What sits in a fruit bowl and shouts for help?
A damson in distress.

What would you do if you had a rubber trumpet?
Join an elastic band.

Why did the bees go on strike?
For shorter flowers and more honey.

What do you feed undernourished dwarfs?
Self-raising flour.

What kind of lighting did Noah have in the Ark?
Flood lighting.

Why don't barbers cut hair any longer?
Because they cut it shorter.

What is an archaeologist?
A man whose career lies in ruins.

Why couldn't the church tower keep a secret?
Because the bells always tolled.

What happened to a man who stole a calendar?
He got twelve months.

Why do white sheep eat more than black sheep?
There are more white sheep.

What would Neptune say if the seas dried up?
I haven't a notion.

What's the difference between an elephant and a biscuit?
You can't dip an elephant in your tea.

Who wears long woolly underwear and sparkles?
Long John Silver.

What did the Leaning Tower of Pisa say to Big Ben?
Let's get together. I've got the inclination, and you've got the time.

Why did the squirrel swim on his back?
To keep his nuts dry.

What did the gas meter say to the shilling?
Glad to see you, bob.

What is the similarity between a debutante and a man with his flies
undone?
They both have coming-out balls.

Why is a plane with a Japanese pilot always cold?
There's a Nip in the air.

What is the difference between Noah's Ark and Joan of Arc?
One was made of wood, the other was Maid of Orleans.

Why is an Indian who has been sat on by an elephant like a crab?
They are both 'crushed Asians'.

Four Jamaicans started up a fried fish shop in London. What was
their telephone number?
Blackfriars 1234.

How do you start a Teddy Bear Race?
Ready, Teddy – Go.

What has two wings and a yellow beak?
A Chinese football team.

Why did the tomato blush?
Because it saw the salad dressing.

Why are tall people lazier than short people?
They're always longer in bed.

What goes up but never comes down?
Your age.

What gets wetter with drying?
A towel.

In rowing you get a crab.
In golf you get a birdie.
In football you get a foul.
What do you get in bowls?
A goldfish.

What's the quickest way to get in touch with a fish?
Just drop him a line.

How can you make your money go a long way?
Send it to the North Pole.

95

What's worse than a giraffe with a sore throat?
A centipede with chilblains.

How can you stop a cock crowing on Monday morning?
Eat him for Sunday dinner.

How do you make a bandstand?
Take away their chairs.

What's yellow and stupid?
Thick custard.

Why does the pony cough?
Because he's a little hoarse.

What's the difference between an old Etonian and Jonah?
One was brought up at Eton, the other was eaten and brought up.

'If there are twenty tomcats and one female cat in a garden, what is
the time?'
'Twenty after one.'

THE HAPPIEST DAYS

There were two deadly rivals at school who hated each other. After they had left their paths never crossed. One became an admiral, the other a bishop. One day there was an important function at Windsor Castle to which they had both been invited. It was a full ceremonial dress affair and they were both on the platform waiting for their train to Windsor. Both were in their full regalia, the admiral in his cocked hat, and the bishop who had become very portly, in his skirt-like black cloak and gaiters.

The bishop suddenly recognised his old rival, so walked up to him and said: 'Excuse me station master, what time does the train for Windsor leave?'

The admiral immediately spotted who it was and replied: 'At one o'clock, madam, but in your present advanced state I would recommend you not to travel.'

A young schoolteacher stooped down to pick up a piece of chalk from the floor. A small boy started to giggle.

'What are you laughing about Johnny?'

'Oh, teacher,' he sniggered. 'I saw your garters.'

'Well go and stand in the corner for an hour,' she snapped.

At that point a boy at the back picked up his satchel, put on his cap and started to leave the classroom.

'Where are you going, Charlie?' asked the teacher.

'Well, if Johnny got one hour in the corner for what *he* saw, after what I saw my schooldays are over,' said Charlie.

Teacher: 'Where are the Virgin Islands?'
Boy: 'I'm not sure, miss. But they must be quite a long way from the Isle of Man.'

The class had been asked to write a short essay on 'The Pleasures of Childhood'. One little boy wrote: 'The pleasures of childhood are great but not to be compared with the pleasures of adultery.'

A young boy arrived late at school.

'Why are you late Johnny?' asked the teacher.

'I'm sorry, miss, but I had to get my own breakfast today.'

'All right, Johnny. Settle down. We are doing geography and here is a map of India and Pakistan. Can you tell me where the Pakistan border is?'

'Yes teacher, in bed with mum. That's why I had to get my own breakfast.'

FOR THE YOUNG

'Who's that at the door?'
'A man with a drum.'
'Tell him to beat it.'

'Do you know the rumour about the pat of butter?'
'No. What is it?'
'I won't tell you. You might spread it.'

'Have you heard the story of the dustbin?'
'No. I haven't.'
'Well. I shouldn't worry. It's just a load of rubbish.'

'Do you know the story of the bed?'
'No. Do tell me.'
'I can't. I haven't made it up yet.'

'Do you know the story of the Manx cat?'
'No. What is it?'
'There's no tail to tell.'

'My car won't go.'
'Is the battery flat?'
'I don't know. What shape should it be?'

'I won't tell you my story about the umbrella.'
'Why not?'
'Because it would be over your head.'

'Willie. Stop playing the piano at once. You know I've told you never to play without first washing your hands.'
'Don't worry mum. I'm only playing the black notes.'

'What are you doing Johnny?'
'I'm writing a letter to my cousin Pat.'
'Don't be silly. You can't write.'
'It doesn't matter. Pat can't read.'

'Willie, if you had £5 in one pocket of your trousers and £2 in the other, what would you have?'
'Someone else's trousers on, teacher.'

'Who's that at the door?'
'A man with a wooden leg.'
'Well, tell him to hop it.'

'Dad, what are you going to do with that manure?'
'Put it on my strawberries, son.'
'That's funny. Mum always gives us sugar and cream.'

Old lady to small boy: 'And what might your name be, young man?'
'It might be Cecil. But it ain't. It's William.'

'I won't tell you my story about the elephant.'
'Why not?'
'You'd never swallow it.'

NAMES TO DROP

The well-known architect **Sir Edward Maufe** arrived late at the reception before a very formal dinner. The toastmaster had given up announcing the guests. So Sir Edward, not wishing to cause any fuss, sidled up to his hostess and murmured his name.

'I'm Maufe,' he said.

'Oh, really,' the hostess replied. 'I'm so sorry you can't stop for the dinner.'

Lord Birkenhead was once buttonholed by a long-winded bore who insisted on recounting at great length the poor treatment which he had received at a certain hotel.

'But, of course,' he concluded. 'As soon as they knew who I was, everything was all right.'

'And *who* were you?' Lord Birkenhead asked politely.

The French government once asked **General de Gaulle** whether he would like a state funeral when he died. He refused, saying it would be a waste of money as he would only be away for three days.

Bernard Shaw was once leaving a party.

'Well, Mr Shaw, I hope you enjoyed yourself,' said his hostess.

'Yes, thank you, madam I did. I was the only thing there was to enjoy.'

A glamorous lady once approached my portrait painter friend the late **Edward Halliday** and asked him if he would paint her in the nude.

'Yes, I will,' he said after a bit of thought. 'But, on one condition. I must keep my socks on. I have to have somewhere to stick my brushes.'

A story is told about the England and Derbyshire fast bowler **Alan Ward**. He once went on a tour of Germany with a club side and, not surprisingly, against an all-German team did the hat-trick. He became known as Jerry Hat-trick Ward.

The **Queen Mother** was once visiting a British hospital in Germany and as usual went up to each bed and talked sympathetically with each man. At one bed, a man was obviously in great pain.
'What's wrong with you?' she asked.
'Oh, ma'am, I've got a terrible boil on my bum.'
The Queen Mother didn't turn a hair but quietly wished the man a quick recovery. When she left the ward the sister came and gave the man a terrible ticking off.
'Never use a word like that in front of royalty. Say anything. Pretend you've sprained your ankle or something. Never do it again.'
The man apologised and agreed that he shouldn't have said it. About six months later Princess Margaret was going round the same hospital on one of her visits as colonel of a regiment. She came into the same ward and the man was still there writhing in pain. When she came to his bed, she asked: 'And what's wrong with you?'
The man remembered what he'd been told by the sister. 'Oh, ma'am,' he said, 'I'm in terrible pain. I've sprained my ankle.'
'Oh, really,' said the princess in some surprise. 'So the boil on your bum is better is it?'

Bernard Shaw and **Winston Churchill** did not get on too well. In the thirties, when Churchill was in the political wilderness, Shaw sent him four tickets for the first night of one of his new plays, adding: 'These are for you and your friends – if you have any.'
Churchill returned the tickets saying he was already engaged on that evening. 'But, I would very much like to have tickets for the second night – if there is one.'

102

When **William Douglas-Home** was at Eton he was asked to write as briefly as possible on either: (1) The Future of Socialism, or (2) The Future of Coal. He chose the second question and wrote just one word: 'Smoke'.

Field-Marshal Lord Montgomery was inspecting a parade of war veterans. He came to a man with only one arm, his other sleeve hanging down empty.

'Where did you get that?' asked Monty.

'Fighting for the 8th Army at the Battle of Alamein, sir,' replied the veteran.

Further up the line was another veteran, also with one empty sleeve.

'And where did you get that?' asked Monty again.

'Fighting for the 8th Army in Sicily, sir,' was the reply.

Each time Monty uttered words of sympathy and encouragement, and recalled the glorious exploits of the 8th Army. Right at the end of the line was a man with no hands showing out of either sleeve.

'Where did you get that?' asked Monty yet again.

'At Burtons, sir. It's going back tomorrow. The sleeves are far too long.'

Lord Reith, the first Director General of the BBC was famous for his puritanical outlook. He required and demanded the highest moral standards from his staff. Woe betide any defaulter. Even the chief engineer was sacked because he told Reith that he was being divorced by his wife. One evening Reith was going round the studios in Broadcasting House and went unexpectedly into one of the drama studios. There, to his horror, was a well-known producer making love to one of the leading actresses in the BBC Repertory *on the table* in the studio.

Reith closed the door quietly and, rushing back to his office, summoned one of his assistants.

'I want you to get rid of the drama producer John Smith and the actress Betty Jones. I have found them making love on a studio table.'

His assistant began to stammer and demur.

'Don't argue,' thundered Reith. 'Get rid of them both *immediately.*'

103

'But, sir,' said the assistant, 'Smith is far and away our best drama producer and Jones our best actress. Furthermore, the play they are rehearsing is already billed in *Radio Times* and goes out next week. It would create an awful scandal if it was cancelled now. The reason would be bound to come out.'

Reith thought for a moment and then made his decision. 'Very well, then. Get rid of the table.'

On Ted Dexter's MCC tour of Australia the manager was the late **Duke of Norfolk**. It was a surprising choice. Dukes are not usually managers of cricket teams. But he was very popular in Australia. They called him Dukey and he endeared himself to them by leasing a racehorse wherever the MCC were playing. When they were playing against South Australia at Adelaide the duke had a horse running at a small country race-course called Gawlor not far from Adelaide. He went to see it run and went down to the paddock to talk to the trainer before the race. The horse was in a far corner under a gum tree, and as the duke strolled across the paddock he saw the trainer take something out of his pocket and give it to the horse to eat. The duke, remembering his position as a member of the Jockey Club and the Queen's representative at Ascot, was worried about dope.

'What's that you have just given the horse to eat?' he asked the trainer anxiously.

'Oh, Your Grace,' replied the trainer looking rather guilty. 'It was just a lump of sugar. In fact I'm going to have one myself. Would you like one too, Your Grace?'

As he spoke the trainer took a lump of sugar out of his pocket and ate it. He then offered another one to the duke who, very much relieved, thought he ought to humour the trainer and took the lump of sugar and put it in his mouth. He then chatted to the trainer and finally began to walk back to the stands. Five minutes before the race the jockeys came into the paddock and the duke's jockey went up to the trainer under the gum tree for his riding instructions.

The trainer told him: 'Listen. This is a 7 furlong race. For the first 5 furlongs keep him on the bit and keep him tucked in behind the others. Then for the last 2 furlongs let him go and give him all you've got. If anyone passes you after that it's either the Duke of Norfolk or myself.'

Someone once wrote an article about the late **Sir Francis Chichester**. There was an accompanying picture under which the caption read: 'Sir Francis Chichester – The great yachtsman who, with his 24 foot cutter, circumcised the world.'

The veteran actor **A.E.Matthews**, who went on acting well into his eighties, used to say: 'I am so old that in the morning my wife brings me up a cup of tea and a copy of *The Times*. I drink the tea, then look at the obituary column in *The Times*. If I'm not in it, I get up.'

A man went up to heaven and reported to St Peter at the pearly gates.

'What's your name, sir?' asked St Peter.

'Johnson,' replied the man.

'Oh yes, we were expecting you. But I'm afraid you haven't done very well down on earth. You'll have to do a year's penance before you become a full member of the Heavenly Host.'

'Oh dear,' said Johnson.'What have I got to do?'

'Well,' said St Peter. 'You see that old crone over there with one tooth, no hair, and a wooden leg. I'm afraid you'll have to live with her for a year.'

'That's a bit tough, but, if you say so, I must do it,' said Johnson, and went over towards the old lady to introduce himself. But, before he could reach her, across a cloud came a cheerful looking **Arthur Scargill** with Raquel Welch on his arm. He, not surprisingly, looked very happy.

So Johnson, in surprise, went back to St Peter and said: 'I say, that's a bit unfair. Look at that Arthur Scargill with that lovely lady. Surely I didn't do worse than him?'

'No. You've got it all wrong,' said St Peter. That's Raquel Welch doing *her* penance.'

Another man approached St Peter.

'Name, please,' said St Peter.

'Geoffrey Boycott,' was the reply.

St Peter ran his finger down his list of names. 'I'm sorry, Mr Boycott. We've got no reservation for you here. You will have to go elsewhere.'

Geoffrey Boycott went off muttering under his breath and came back after a few minutes.

'Excuse me. I don't think you could have heard me all right just now. I am Geoffrey Boycott, late of Yorkshire and England.'

'I'm sorry, sir. We still haven't got a place for you.'

As Boycott walked off, a very old man with a long grey beard walked up to the gates.

'Yes, sir?' said St Peter.

'I am Geoffrey Boycott,' said the old man. 'Can I come in?'

'Certainly sir,' said St Peter. 'Welcome. We're very glad to see you.'

A man who had been waiting his turn asked St Peter why he had turned away the real Geoffrey Boycott and had then immediately welcomed the old man who was obviously only pretending.

'Well, you see the old man is God and we have to humour him. He keeps on thinking he's Geoffrey Boycott,' replied St Peter.

Groucho Marx was once taken to lunch in a very posh New York club. He praised the excellent food and his host said: 'Well, why don't you become a member? I'm sure the committee would be honoured and delighted to elect you.'

'No,' said Groucho. 'Thank you for your kind thought, but I would never want to belong to a club which would have me as a member.'

During the American Civil War **General Sedgemore** was inspecting his front line. He was a brave man and ignored warnings from his junior officers not to put his head over the parapet to see the enemy's positions.

'It's quite safe,' he said, as he stuck his head over the top. 'They couldn't hit an elephant at the dis . . . '.

In the early thirties **King Abadulla of Jordan** was the guest of King George V and Queen Mary at a banquet in Buckingham Palace. When the meal started, a royal flunkey brought an enormous tureen of soup to the top table. He helped Queen Mary and was about to give some to King Abadulla when the latter said loudly: 'No thank you. No soup for me. It makes me fart.'

106

There was consternation among the royal guests, until King Abadulla went on, patting his enormous stomach: 'Look,' he said. 'I am fa(r)t enough already.'

A FEW EXTRAS

A man walked into his local town hall and asked the porter at reception if he could see the man in charge of pubic affairs.

'Surely you mean public affairs, sir?' said the porter.

'No,' said the man. 'This is a private matter.'

A young man was doing some energetic press-ups on the beach. An old lady was watching him for about ten minutes and then went up to him and tapped him on the shoulder.

'Excuse me, young man,' she said, 'I think you ought to know that the young lady – or whoever it was – has been gone for over ten minutes.'

George Robey used to tell the story of the businessman who was asked for a good tip on the Stock Exchange by a young man. After a moment's thought the businessman replied: 'If I were you, I would put all you've got into rubber. And if it comes off, marry the girl.'

A man was driving slowly across an open-country level-crossing when a train came hurtling around the bend at 90 miles an hour.

'How did the man in the car get across?'

'His widow gave him one.'

Two people were trying to do a crossword puzzle. The one reading out the clues asked:

'An over-burdened postman?'

'How many letters?' asked his friend.

'Hundreds of them,' was the reply.

Man on telephone:
'Is that the Salvation Army?'
'Yes.'
'Do you save girls?'
'Yes, we certainly try to.'
'Well, save one for me on Saturday night.'

A Teddy Boy sat down in a hairdresser's chair.
'Hair cut, sir?' asked the barber.
'No. Just change the oil.'

A man jumped off a sky-scraper and miraculously fell unhurt on to the pavement. As he got up and brushed himself down, a passer-by rushed up to him and asked: 'What happened?'
'I don't know,' was the reply. 'I've only just arrived.'

A man smoked evil-smelling cigars. His friends called them Adam and Eve cigars. Every time he Adam, they Eved.

Two old ladies were sitting in deckchairs watching a first-class cricket match. Suddenly a streaker ran across the field towards them. He was a fine specimen of a man. The ladies got very excited as they saw this magnificent figure approaching. As he ran right past their chairs, one of the old ladies had a stroke – the other couldn't reach him.

A young man and his girlfriend were riding a tandem bicycle. They came to the bottom of a steep hill, and the young man said: 'Get off. We're going to shove it up here.'
'Suits me,' said the girl, 'but what shall we do with the bike?'

The food at a cricket club dinner was not up to standard. One of the members wrote to the secretary to complain.
'I'm so sorry you didn't enjoy your meal,' wrote back the secretary.
'Will you please bring it up at the annual general meeting.'

109

The treasurer of a club sent a letter round to members saying that the annual subscription would have to go up to £5 per annum. Unfortunately, his secretary couldn't spell and left out one of the 'n's in annum. A member wrote back deploring the treasurer's letter, saying that he would prefer to continue paying *through the nose*.

A guest sitting at the top table at a club dinner got hardly any wine to drink all evening. But he got his own back. He was down to propose the health of Absent Friends and he coupled this with the name of the wine waiter.

A man was looking very down in the mouth and his friend asked him what was the matter.
  'Oh,' he replied. 'I'm very worried about the 3Ms.'
  '3Ms?' asked his friend. 'What on earth do you mean?'
  'Well,' was the reply. 'It's the missus, the maid and the mortgage. They are all three overdue.'

There was a bank raid and the raiders told all the staff to lie face down on the floor. They all did so at once except for an attractive cashier, who lay on her back.
  'Miss Allardyce,' whispered the man next to her. 'Do as you are told. Lie on your tummy, face down. This is a genuine stick-up, not the annual audit.'

A desert patrol was lost in a sandstorm. They wandered about for several days and had soon finished the meagre rations which they had brought with them. The officer addressed his men.
  'I've got two bits of news for you, one bad, one good. The bad news is that our rations have run out and that from now on we shall have to eat camel dung. The good news is that there's plenty of it.'

A man applied for a job as a wood-cutter on a large country estate.
  'Where did you learn your trade?' asked the farm manager.
  'In the Sahara,' replied the man.

110

'But there aren't any trees in the Sahara,' snapped the farmer.
'Not now there aren't,' replied the man.

A small man and his very large wife went on to the pier at Blackpool and decided to try the talking weighing machine. The man put his penny in the slot and got on to the machine. A voice from inside it announced: '10 stone 1 lb.'

Then it was the wife's turn. When she got on, the machine spoke out: 'One at a time please.'

A man once reckoned that he was so unlucky that if he had been one of Raquel Welch's triplets, he'd have been the one that was bottle fed.

The Quiz Master asked: 'What were the first words that Eve said to Adam when she saw him in the Garden of Eden?'

The young lady contestant thought for a moment, and shook her head. 'That's a hard one,' she said to the Quiz Master.

He replied: 'Quite right. Two marks.'

A man went into a pub.

'Good evening, sir,' said the landlord. 'What would you like to drink?'

'A large whisky, thank you.'

The landlord said: 'That will be 90p please.'

'Oh, no,' said the man. 'I distinctly remember you inviting me to have a drink. I thought it was very kind of you.'

The landlord turned to another customer, who was a solicitor, and asked for support. The solicitor said that he was sorry, but the landlord had definitely made an offer and the man had accepted it, so, he did not have to pay. The landlord was furious and turned the man out of the pub, telling him never to come back again. But about ten minutes later the man reappeared.

'I thought I told you never to come back,' said the landlord.

'I've never been here before in my life,' said the man.

'Then you must have a double,' said the landlord.

'Thank you very much, I will, and I'm sure our solicitor friend would like one two.'

The rich lady returned from a ball and rang the bell for her footman and said: 'Edward, take off my shoes,' and he did. Then she said: 'Edward, take off my coat,' and he did. 'Take off my dress,' and he did. 'And now take off my underclothes,' and he did. 'And now, Edward,' she said, 'if you wish to remain in my service, you are never to wear any of my clothes again.'

Three elderly men were discussing how they would like to die.
1st old man: 'I would like to die after planting a flag on the top of Everest.'
2nd old man: 'I would like to die after taking a wicket with the last ball of a test match, and so winning the test for England.'
3rd old man: 'I would like to die in bed – shot by a jealous husband.'

Speaker at a dinner: 'Can you hear me at the back of the room?'
A voice: 'Yes I can. But I will willingly swop with someone who can't.'

The after-dinner speaker went on and on. Finally, a guest got so fed up that he picked up a bottle and threw it at the speaker's head. Unfortunately the bottle hit a small man sitting at the top table. People rushed to his assistance and finally brought him round. As he came to he murmured: 'Please hit me again. I can still hear him.'

The local squire and his wife were entertaining their tenants and servants to a Christmas party. The conjuror, whom they had engaged, approached an elderly gamekeeper type.
'Would you be surprised if I brought a live rabbit out of your inside pocket?' he asked the gamekeeper.
'That I would be,' growled the gamekeeper. 'I've got a ruddy ferret in there.'

During the war at a medical centre, a man failed his eyesight test because he said he couldn't even read the top line of the letters' chart. The eye specialist was a bit suspicious, but had to certify the man as unfit for active service. By chance, on his way home that evening, the specialist dropped in at the newsreel cinema. To his amazement he saw in the row in front of him the man whom he had just failed for bad eyesight. He leaned forward and tapped the man on the shoulder.

'Haven't I seen you somewhere recently?' he asked.

The man turned round and recognised the specialist. 'Ah, kind sir,' he said. 'Could you tell me, does this bus go to Victoria?'

A young, recently married man was a member of his local Round Table. Once a month they had a meeting when the newer members had to address the other members on a subject which was drawn out of a hat. He drew out 'sex', and proceeded to give a masterly discourse on the subject based on his new experiences as a married man. When he got home he told his wife that he had had to make a speech, but was too bashful to say what the subject was. So when she asked him, he said: 'Oh, er . . . yachting.'

The next day the young wife went into her bank and the manager came forward and said how excellent her husband had been, with such an expert knowledge of his subject.

'That's funny,' she said. 'He's only done it twice. The first time he was sick. The second time his hat flew off.'

A professor was doing research into the sex life of the average married male. A special meeting was arranged for him to which married men of all ages were invited. He had a packed house and explained what he was doing.

'To start with,' he said, 'I wonder whether any of you who make love to your wife *every* night will stand up.'

Quite a number of the younger members of the audience stood up. The professor counted them and then asked anyone who did it every *other* night to stand up. This continued for some time, with those who did it three times a week, twice a week, once a week, and once a month.

Satisfied by the response the professor thanked everyone and said: 'Well, I reckon that includes you all. Thank you for your help.'

But at the back of the room a small man meekly held up his hand. He had a happy face and was smiling broadly.

'Please sir,' he said, 'You haven't asked me. I do it once a year.'

'Well, what have you got to look so cheerful about?' asked the professor.

The little man smiled even more and said: 'It's tonight.'

The popular pianist at a pub had retired and the landlord put up a notice advertising the job. One day a dirty-looking tramp came in. His clothes were in tatters and there was an enormous hole in the seat of his trousers. He saw the piano in the corner and immediately went over, sat in the wicker chair in front of it and started to play. He played beautifully, modern tunes, old tunes, classics – the lot. The customers began to gather round, applauding him and asking for their special favourites to be played. He seemed to know all the requests, but if he wasn't sure he just asked the customer to sing the opening few bars and he soon picked it up. The landlord was delighted, took him a pint of beer, and in spite of his terrible clothes and the hole in his trousers, decided to give him the job. The requests continued to flow in until a little old lady, who had been sitting quietly sipping a port and lemon, approached the tramp and tapped him on the shoulder.

'Do you know,' she whispered confidentially, 'your balls are hanging through the wicker chair?'

'No, I don't madam,' said the tramp. 'But, if you'll hum it, I'll soon be able to play it.'

A lady was on the towpath watching the two university crews practising at Putney the day before the boat race. She approached one of the BBC commentators and said: 'Excuse me troubling you, but I'm a great enthusiast of the boat race and come to watch it every year. But can you please explain to me why the two same crews are always in the final?'

The hotel guest wanted a clean towel, so rang the bell which said 'maid'. He rang and rang and after a long delay an elderly porter knocked on his door.

'I've been ringing for ages. Where's the chambermaid?' the guest asked angrily.

'I'm not sure, sir. But I think it comes from the Potteries.'

A farmer was having great trouble with hikers walking across his land. So he put up a notice on the gate to one of his fields: 'Trespassers admitted free. The bull will charge you later.'

A man was making a house to house collection on behalf of the Brighouse and Rastrick Brass Band Instrument Purchase and Repair Fund. He rang the bell of a house which belonged to a crotchety old spinster, who in spite of being well off was notoriously mean. His friends had told him he didn't have a chance with her, but he thought he would have a try just the same. He had to ring several times and after a long delay the door was slightly opened and the old lady asked him what he wanted.

'Madam. I am collecting on behalf of the Brighouse and Rastrick Brass Band Instrument Purchase and Repair Fund. I wonder if you would be so generous as to give something?'

The old lady cupped her ear and said: 'Speak up. I can't hear a word. What did you say?'

So the man repeated very loudly what he had said.

Still the old lady shook her head and said: 'It's no use. You must speak even louder.'

So this time he shouted at the top of his voice but with no result.

The old lady shook her head and made as if to close the door.

'Stingy old bitch,' muttered the man quietly under his breath. 'As far as I am concerned you can get stuffed.'

'In that case,' said the old lady, 'you too can stuff your Brighouse and Rastrick Brass Band Instrument Purchase and Repair Fund' – and slammed the door.

A Chinaman was stopped by an interviewer and asked which television he preferred – BBC or ITV. He refused to answer. The interviewer asked him why.

'Me no telly,' he replied.

An artist was embracing his attractive young model. Suddenly he heard his wife coming up the stairs.

'Quick,' he said 'Take your clothes off at once – I'm supposed to be working.'

115

A very rich Arab sheik was staying in a small country hotel. It was the only accommodation he could get at short notice and his room didn't even have a washbasin. During the night his servant slept on the floor in the corridor outside his room. Twice the sheik called out and woke him to go and get a glass of water. Early in the morning he called out again for yet another glass. After five minutes' delay the servant returned, knocked on the door and entered with an empty glass.

'Where's my water?' demanded the sheik.

'I'm sorry master. I waited a few minutes. But Big White Chief sit on well.'

An English farmer was showing an Australian sheep farmer round his farm. They travelled in his Land Rover and the journey round the 500 acres or so took almost half an hour. When they got back to the farmhouse the Englishman asked the Australian what he thought about the farm.

'Well, way back in Australia, I can get in my car and it will take me four days to go round *my* estate.'

'Yes, I sympathise,' said the Englishman. 'I once had a car like that.'

An old lady was being shown round the gardens of an old house on the Isle of Purbeck in Dorset. The district is famous for its fossils of dinosaur foot marks and, sure enough, this garden had two perfect specimens. The owner proudly pointed them out to the old lady.

'Look at these dinosaur's foot prints,' she said. 'You can tell how big they must have been.'

'Yes,' said the old lady. 'They're wonderful. And to think that they came so close to the house.'

Early one morning a young man took a girl for a walk in the fields. The sun was up and the grass was damp. He knelt down to test it.

'Some dew,' he said.

'Some don't,' she said, 'Good morning.'

'Do you believe in clubs for women?'

'No. I always try kindness first.'

116

A man was staying in the country for the weekend and was sitting on the sun terrace with his hostess. Some pigeons flew overhead and one dropped a 'message' on the man's smart blue blazer.

'Oh, dear,' said his hostess. 'I'll go and get a bit of loo paper.'

'I shouldn't worry,' said the man. 'By the time you get back the pigeon will be miles away.'

A man in a factory had an accident with one of the machines. But he didn't realise that he had lost two fingers until he was about to say goodnight to the foreman.

A young man lived next door to his girlfriend and one winter night was kissing her goodnight on her doorstep. He suddenly wanted to spend a penny and his girlfriend suggested that he did it in the snow, which was lying thick on the ground. Next day her father called on the boy's father. He complained that the boy had spent a penny on the lawn, spelling out his name as he did it. The neighbours were all leaning over his wall and pointing to it, and it was very embarrassing.

'Oh, I shouldn't take it too seriously,' said the boy's father. 'Boys will be boys and I can't really see much harm in what he has done.'

'Maybe you can't, but I can,' said the girl's father. 'The trouble is, his name is written in my daughter's handwriting.'

An elderly lady had been told by her doctor to go away and recuperate after a severe operation. So she booked into a small hotel in the German mountains, where she would get peace and quiet. She wrote to the manager to check where the WC was, as she did not want it too far from her room. The German manager did not know what WC stood for. So he went to check with the local schoolmaster, who spoke good English.

'WC,' said the schoolmaster. 'That's easy. It's short for Weslyan Chapel.'

So the manager wrote back to the lady with the help of the schoolmaster:

Dear Madam,
In answer to your question, the WC is situated about 7 miles away in

the middle of a forest, amid lovely surroundings. It's open on Sundays, Thursdays, and Fridays. This is unfortunate if you are in the habit of going regularly. But a number of people take their lunch with them and make a day of it. Others, who cannot spare the time, go by car and arrive at the last moment, as they are in a great hurry and cannot wait.

The accommodation is good and there are twenty seats. But, should you be late, there is plenty of standing room. I would advise you to pay a visit on Thursday, when there is an organ accompaniment. The acoustics are excellent, even the most delicate sounds can be heard.

I shall be delighted to accompany you and show you round, and if you wish will reserve a special seat for you.

Yours faithfully,

PS 1 Hymn sheets are supplied at the church door.
PS 2 My wife and I have not been for eight months, which pains us greatly.

Lady on a Middle East cruise: 'Steward, can you please tell me where the nearest toilet is?'
Steward; 'Yes, madam. Port side.'
Lady: 'Good gracious. I can't possibly last that long.'

Jimmy James was one of my favourite comedians. He kept a dead-pan face, puffed continuously at cigarettes, and had a stuttering walk, 'giving' occasionally at the knees. One of his stooges was called Eli, and Jimmy used to tell him that he had plans for him to become an intrepid parachutist. Eli would be flown 20,000 feet above the theatre and would then drop through the roof of the theatre.

'Don't pull the rip-cord until you are ten feet above the stalls.'
'But what will happen if the parachute doesn't open?' asked Eli.
'You can jump ten feet can't you?' was Jimmy's reply.

Three men were waiting at the gates of heaven, and St Peter was checking them in. He asked the first man what had been the cause of his death.

'I got home early one night and found a man in bed with my wife. He jumped out of the window and tried to escape down the fire-escape. So I threw the fridge out of the window hoping it would hit him. I suppose the sudden exertion must have brought on a heart attack.'

'Right,' said St Peter, and asked the second man: 'Your cause of death please?'

'A blow from a falling heavy object.'

'And the cause of your death?' St Peter asked the third man.

'Well, I don't really know,' he replied. 'There I was sitting innocently in this fridge . . .'

Two MPs were talking in the tea-room of the House of Commons.

'I'm not sure what to do about the Abortion Bill. What do you think I should do?'

'Oh, pay it at once, before someone finds out,' his companion replied.

He was a single man with a double chin and a treble voice. He lived in a very poor district. The sort of place where if you don't pay the rent they put you into prison. But, if you *do* pay, the police come round to ask where you got the money.

Billy Bennett used to say that his brother had a single hair on the end of his nose. It was so long that everytime he sneezed it cracked like a whip. One day he took a large dose of snuff and nearly flogged himself to death.

I'm going to sing:

The motoring song – Four wheel break the news to mother.

The petrol song – Shell Oil acquaintance be forgot.

The omnivorous song – Omnivorous happy as when I'm with you.

A man accidentally leaned against a bacon slicer in a grocer's shop. As a result some of the customers got a little behind with their orders.

119

A woman was complaining to her butcher about some sausages which she had bought.

'They had meat at one end and bread at the other.'

'I am sorry madam,' said the butcher. 'But in these hard times it's difficult to make both ends meet.'

A lady walked into a butcher's shop and said to the man in the straw hat behind the counter: 'Do you keep dripping?'

He replied: 'No, madam. Not since I've had it fixed.'

A man who lived next door to a pub had a favourite tabby cat. Unfortunately the cat was run over by a car and killed. A year later at about midnight the publican was doing his accounts. Suddenly the ghost of this cat appeared in front of him, holding half his tail in his hand.

'Can you help me please?' said the cat's ghost. 'I expect you remember me when I lived next door. My old master has moved, so I thought I would try you.'

'Yes, I do remember you,' said the publican. 'You were a nice cat. What can I do for you?'

'Well,' said the cat's ghost. 'You see this bit of tail which I am holding in my hand? It was cut off in my accident and I'm fed up carrying it around with me. Can you mend it for me please?'

'I'm sorry,' said the publican, 'much as I would like to, I cannot help you. I'm not allowed to retail spirits after eleven o'clock.'

You See What I Mean
Definitions

A Baby – nine months interest on a small deposit.

A Ball-race – tomcat with 20 yards' start on the vet.

Board of Trade – a bench in the park.

A Busybody – a prostitute.

Chivalry – a man's inclination to protect a woman from every man but himself.

Kiss – application on the top floor for a job in the basement.

Metallurgist – one who can look at a platinum blonde and tell whether she is virgin metal or common ore.

Mistress – something between a mister and a mattress.

Mother's Day – nine months after Father's Night.

Out-door Girl – one with the bloom of youth in her cheeks and the cheeks of youth in her bloomers.

Pyjamas – items of clothing which newly weds place by the bed in case of fire.

A Queer – a man who likes his vice versa.

Spring – when a young man's fancy turns to what a woman has been thinking of all the winter.

Taxidermist – a man who mounts animals.

Twins – womb-mates who become bosom pals.

Words Failed Them

The following are actual statements found on insurance forms where car drivers attempted to summarise the details of an accident in the fewest possible words.

Coming home I drove into the wrong house and collided with a tree I don't have.

The other car collided with mine without giving warning of its intention.

I thought my window was down, but I found out it was up when I put my head through it.

I collided with a stationary truck coming the other way.

I pulled away from the side of the road, glanced at my mother-in-law and headed over the embankment.

In an attempt to kill a fly, I drove into a telephone pole.